waking up

up

with

everyone

around us

TEJ STEINER

Waking Up With Everyone Around Us

by Tej Steiner

© 2017 Tej Steiner

www.tejsteiner.com

Published by Heart Circle Network, LLC

Ashland, Oregon

www.heartcircle.com

Design: Book Savvy Studio

Editing: Mary Londos and

Copyediting: Kathryn Thomas

ISBN: 978-0692907092

First Edition

Printed in the United States of America

CONTENTS

Part I

WAKING UP

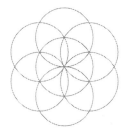

The coming times are already here. The old ways are collapsing to make room for the new. The breakdown in the trends and patterns that have defined our lives can easily produce instability and fear. To truly meet these times, we need the wisdom of several million saints.

Fortunately, plenty of saints have signed up for this, more than enough to handle the job.

What we really need now are circles for the saints to sit in—supportive environments to greet and meet each other; places to huddle together so we can come up with the next play.

• • •

A radically new kind of teacher is just beginning to show up in today's world: the circle-teacher. I am one of those teachers. As such, while I'm interested in practices and teachings that support Heart Awakening and individual transformation, this is not my primary passion. My primary passion is exploring how we can change our existing social groups and relationships so that they support individual transformation. For forty years, I've studied and taught what I call *Transformational Group Dynamics*. This is about how we can re-organize our own families, schools, friendships, marriages, businesses, prisons, governments, spiritual groups, churches, temples, non-profit organizations, and political parties so that they become social environments that encourage Heart Awakening rather than environments that discourage it.

I'm writing this book to share with you what I've learned. It's divided into two distinct sections:

Waking Up: In the first half of the book, I offer a practical way of understanding what awakening is, so we have a more accurate framework or heart-map to better awaken with. It cuts across all belief systems, spiritual disciplines, and cultural differences. It is non-proscriptive and non-directive, so that we maintain full freedom to follow our own way to Heart Awakening.

With Everyone Around Us: In the second half of the book, I present an entirely new way of looking at groups and relationships so that we have a better way of understanding how they can become "awakening-friendly." I then give a detailed, practical process through which we can re-organize any group we're in so that it supports Heart Awakening. I call this process *Heart Circle*.

If you are interested in personal and social transformation, I think you'll enjoy reading this book as much as I have enjoyed writing it.

YOUR TIME OF HIDING

We found the crown
You had hidden so well
And we placed it on your head today.
Your time of hiding is over.

Those countless years
Spent in the crowded market place
Posing as a buyer
Of day-old bread
And spoiled fruit
Have passed.
It's time to sit upon your throne again.

You have suffered enough.
You have died more times
Than you can remember.
Your heart is ready to rule.

We're not asking for your opinion about this.

1

HEART AWAKENING
An Overview

My Story

I was born in the United States at a perfect time to be drafted into the army during the height of the Vietnam War. In 1969, I was twenty-one. My college career had been cut short in my junior year when I was expelled from school for leading a peaceful anti-war demonstration at the University of Kansas. Kansas was a pretty conservative place at the time. Still is, actually. Being against the war, I chose to go to Canada rather than Vietnam. I hitchhiked from my hometown of St. Louis, Missouri, up into Canada, over the Great Lakes, and down to Toronto, Ontario. I arrived with a pack on my back, with very little money, knowing absolutely no one.

My World War II Marine Corps father thought I was a communist for leaving the country. I wasn't; I just felt that the war was wrong. Some people thought I was a coward, afraid of fighting. Others thought I was a traitor. My brother Jim, a Marine Vietnam veteran himself, thought I was courageous. He had already seen the senseless carnage going on in Vietnam and was glad I made the decision to not add to it.

For me, the decision wasn't about being courageous or cowardly. It wasn't about morality or being a pacifist. I simply wasn't going to kill Vietnamese people. It felt absurd to me, as absurd as if someone had ordered me to kill our next-door neighbors, the Schuberts. "What do you mean, go kill the Schuberts? Are you nuts? They're my neighbors! If you try to force me to kill them, I'll leave the neighborhood. I'll go to Canada where people have nothing against the Schuberts."

The decision to leave my country was incredibly difficult. I knew my chances of ever coming back were small. It meant leaving my family and friends, as well as my identity as an American. I was raised as a kind of All-American boy: class president, athlete, student council member, and honor student. In high school, I was voted "Most Likely to Become President." Leaving the United States turned me into an All-American boy without a country. Although I smile at this now, it was confusing back then. Still, I was willing to leave everything, given that the alternative wasn't an option. But I left, with great sadness, and even greater uncertainty as to where my decision would lead. I also felt terribly alone.

I arrived in Canada in the center of downtown Toronto on a bright, beautiful autumn day. As soon as I got out of the car and looked around, I felt something totally unexpected. It was as if I had come home! Toronto was alive, vibrant, cosmopolitan, friendly, relaxed, and unwar-like. I fell in love with the city and, later, with Canada as a country.

It was in Toronto, a year after my arrival, that I had my first glimpse of Heart Awakening. It happened simply enough. I had started a community center in the downtown area that helped newly arriving draft resisters and deserters find new friends, housing, and jobs. I was up late talking with a fellow draft resister on a warm August night. I don't remember what we were talking about but, all of a sudden, he got quiet for a moment and, seemingly out of the blue, leaned over to me and said, "Tej, the struggle's over." Surprised, I asked, "What do you mean, the struggle's over?" And he just repeated, "The struggle's over, Tej."

I have no idea why he said this. I don't think he knew either. He was as surprised as I was about the effect his pronouncement had on me. Some essential part in me instantly relaxed. I felt a surge of energy throughout my body. For whatever reason, what he said set off a light-filled explosion within me. I opened into what felt like a completely different reality. Everything became one thing.

Before that moment there had been me and then everything else outside of me. But in one unexpected instant, there was no longer an "outside of me." Everything linked up into wholeness. No seams. No "you and me." No God separate from creation. Just Oneness. I felt ecstatic, empathic, peaceful, and empowered. It was as if I'd been seeing life in black and white, and now suddenly everything was filled with vibrant color. As if I had been insane my whole life, now suddenly I was sane.

My first response was to laugh in utter joy. After a minute or two my laughter turned to deep sobbing, the kind that comes with profound gratitude and indescribable relief. Then the laughter started again until the crying and laughter were indistinguishable.

I had no context for this experience. I had heard something about awakening, but I didn't know that's what this was and I didn't know whether anyone else had ever experienced it before.

During the next three days, my perception of life changed dramatically. I found myself loving people I hadn't particularly liked before; I loved everybody. Energy was running through my hands and body. Life made complete sense. I glimpsed that we are all alive in order to consciously feel the vastness of who we are, rather than to live in the tiny, limited version of who we think we are.

For me, accessing this awareness was the answer to all personal and social problems. Feeling connected to everything, I could never harm another person. Stealing would be robbing myself. Depression and other mental disorders had nothing to latch onto. Being a billionaire when others had little didn't seem right or wrong, simply grotesque and silly. War could easily turn into contests to see who could forgive each other first. I saw that families, schools, and businesses could become functional and fulfilling when the people within them felt connected to one another. More than anything else, I experienced a grand perfection in everything. The idea that something was a miracle and something else wasn't seemed comical. That all things came to exist out of nothingness made everything a miracle.

I was astounded by the mere existence of air, fire, toes, or music. Magnificent color was everywhere, especially the deep blues and greens of sky and earth. Trees, once inanimate objects to me, became living, breathing, majestic beings with intelligence and rooted patience. Children recognized that I saw them. Dogs and cats told me their secrets. I was having a great time!

Then on the fourth day, it all crashed back to "normal." Just as suddenly as I had come into feeling Oneness, I went back into feeling separate from everything. It was hell. Pure hell. I knew then what hell actually was: disconnection. And I was in it. Not only had I not known that Oneness existed, I also didn't know that I could be expelled from feeling it once I had experienced it.

But expelled I was. The doors closed with a bang and I didn't know how to re-open them. I didn't know who to talk to about my loss. I knew it wasn't about religion. I wasn't using drugs. Philosophy didn't seem relevant. There was nothing to verify the reality of my experience. I had no teachers. It was excruciatingly confusing to me.

At the same time, as painful as this was, I knew I had found my life purpose. It was to find a way back into the heart connection I had just experienced for three glorious days.

I began my search. I had to get back "there," without knowing where "there" was.

In 1970, personal transformation, Heart Awakening, and expanded awareness were just beginning to make their way into Western culture.

Back then, we were still confusing yoga with yogurt; both were new on the scene. Few people knew anything about meditation, the healing arts, or Oneness. Now, almost fifty years later, information and support for Heart Awakening are everywhere. We have an increasingly common vocabulary for it. There are hundreds of thousands of teachers, practices, and publications that in some way contribute to our personal awakening.

My quest led me to study with what turned into a long list of teachers. I experimented in depth with Kundalini yoga, special diets, different religions, and many self-help practices.

In some ways, I did it all. I was the proverbial seeker, climbing up the mountain to find out what the guy at the top had to say and then rolling back down the mountain, only to climb up another mountain to do it all over again.

During these years, I began to see life through the lens of my search. I slowly developed an overview that made increasing sense to me. I also saw history in a new way, which takes us to the next chapter. Two versions of history are converging right now as you read this.

Two Different Lovers

Like everybody else
You have a choice between two lovers.
One lover is called *Now.*
She has a joyful story
She wants to whisper in your ear.
It's a story you've never heard before.

You can also choose another lover.
Her name is *Time.*
She too will whisper in your ear
But her story is never new.
You've heard it before
Over
And over
And over
Again.

Time will tell you
That you're young and strong
That you're bold and beautiful
Endlessly special
And in control of everything
Including her.
She's quite convincing.

But then
With no warning at all
She'll just drop you.
In a flash

She'll be gone.
You won't know where she went
Or why she left you.
You will feel betrayed and shaken
Like a dead leaf
Floating down a river that doesn't care.

You can cry, scream, and yell in despair
Punch a hole in the wall if you want.
Won't matter.
Once *Time's* gone
She's never coming back.
She's just like that.

But don't worry.
You're not alone.
She does this to everybody.

There's a trick here, of course.
It's a simple truth
But hard to follow.

Don't mess with *Time.*
Treat *Now* like she's all there is.

That's it!

Choose to love *Now*
Before *Time* runs out ...

2

TWO HISTORIES MERGING

External and Internal History

If you were raised in the West, you were probably exposed to what I call "external history." It's almost exclusively a white, male-centric history that deals with facts, dates, and chronological events. It centers around different civilizations: their rising and falling, their social customs, technological advancements, wars, and leaders.

In an historical nutshell, we learned about the Egyptians and their pyramids, the Greeks in Sparta and Athens, the Romans with their world empire, followed by some Dark Ages and the rise of colonizing nation states in Europe. The New World was discovered, as if no one had been living there at the time. Thus, the story goes, America came into being. Slavery started in the U.S. and a civil war ended it. Women got to vote. Hitler happened. Communists came and went. The New York Trade Towers were blown up on 9/11. And here we are today with much of the world at war, this time with invisible enemies like terrorists, tyranny, viruses, drugs, wildfires, and weather.

Within this chronological, linear version of history, there's also the story of scientific achievements: first was fire, then stone tools, the wheel, and of course, the almighty wooden or bone club that morphed into better and better weapons, like AK-47s and nuclear bombs. There was the plow, the clock, the printing press, electricity, computers, and a million technological upgrades which all lead to the sense that science and more information can fix anything. While this quick summary is a bit of an over-generalized version of external history, it went something like that.

There is another altogether different history normally not taught in schools. It's a parallel history that helps make sense of external history. It's not about facts, dates, and events. Instead, it's the history of our own evolving human awareness. I call it "internal history."

Internal history is the evolutionary story of how our awareness and perception have changed and continue to change over time. It is about who we experience ourselves to be and why we are here sailing around the sun on this beautiful little planet. It is the history in which you and I are full participants, rather than just observers of external timelines and events. It's a history that exists both inside and outside of time. It can be told in just a few paragraphs. However, to understand it in such an abbreviated form requires your own evolved awareness. Without your awareness, it won't make sense. But with it, what's written here will seem obvious. It will be what you already know, stated in another way.

This history of human consciousness centers around one key term: Heart Awakening. As I'm defining it, Heart Awakening refers to a transformational leap in perception that results in two fundamental changes in how we experience life. First, it involves a shift out of the perception that we are individuals disconnected from life, into the perception that we are connected to the whole of life. This majestic connection is not based upon a belief, but rather on the ongoing, moment-to-moment, direct experience of our connection. It isn't about religion or philosophy, because belief and intellectual understanding are not needed in order to awaken; in fact, they often get in the way.

The second fundamental change that defines Heart Awakening is opening into an inexplicable, abiding love for everything and everyone. It is the development and deepening of human empathy—our ability to feel into and care for what others are experiencing. It also comes with a profound longing to stay inside the experience of connection rather than return to the misperception of feeling existentially alone.

In our internal history, we started out experiencing ourselves as un-differentiated beings, living within a collective-tribal consciousness. The individual was not distinct from the tribe. There was little sense of an individualistic "I." There are still pockets of indigenous people today living within this less-differentiated state.

Through a miraculous evolutionary process, we slowly began individuating. As a species, we became aware of ourselves as distinct, separate identities. But there was a price to pay for individuation. Most of us lost the experience of being connected to the whole. Being separate and different from everything outside of our bodies, we could no longer feel our interwoven connection with everything. On one hand, we are obviously not the tree. On the other hand, Trees R Us.

While it's an evolutionary imperative to evolve from a tribal collective consciousness into a distinct ego-awareness consciousness, it's the loss of feeling connected to the whole that ends up creating suffering, scarcity, conflict, and—more than anything else—fear that "I" will die. In this separated state, we often become existentially afraid of life itself. We then organize our lives individually and collectively around survival and control.

Over the same evolutionary arc, thinking turned out to be our most important adaptation for physical survival. Individuation came as we developed our capacity to think. Evolution demanded that we develop our rational minds so we could out-think the claws, jaws, and speed of the tiger. We had to control nature by growing food and domesticating animals rather than relying on the hunt. We had to think of better ways to compete with our hostile neighbor's intent. We had to think our way through problems that would destroy us if we didn't come up with a plan. The competitive edge we had over every other species was our ability to think, reason, and then communicate with one another.

This evolutionary imperative forced us to create the necessary mental brilliance that led us to where we are today. Using rational thought, our average human life span increased from thirty years to eighty years. We cured ourselves of many diseases. We carved leisure time out of survival time. We got plenty to eat and built warm houses in cold climates. We ended up having a much better time in life by playing golf, buying stuff, reading books, entering our poodle in a kennel club show, and surfing the Internet. We survived and thrived. We made it here.

The only catch was that during these thousands of productive years, we also became more and more dominated by our own constant thinking. We got a little over-differentiated. It happens.

As we developed the rational part of our brains, we diminished our capacities of empathy, compassion, love, wonder, cooperation, understanding, intuition, connection, and joy. These qualities aren't accessible by thinking our way into them.

Over the centuries, the people with the most developed left hemispheres and rational thinking tendencies were the ones who survived best. They were in control. It was natural selection at work. We developed cultures where the conceptual-mind people dominated the experiential-heart people. The cleverest people with more left-brain power eventually dominated the ones with less.

As the centuries passed, this dominance became more and more absolute. We created sophisticated technology. The people in charge of government, military, production, information, education, finance, entertainment, health, and religion were mostly left-brain dominators, the ones who brought us a bright, but flawed idea: "I think, therefore I am." They were the problem solvers who got the job done. They built the roads, the bridges, and the electrical grid. They declared the wars, made up the religions, and collected the taxes. Alexander the Great, Caesar Augustus, Genghis Kahn, Christopher Columbus, Andrew Jackson, Joseph Stalin, and our other iconic dominators were in charge. As victors, they wrote the history, which conveniently left out the fact that some of them were sociopaths. Slaughtering a million people wasn't a problem for them.

During all of these years, the vast majority of people within any given culture and time period—be they Greek, Roman, Chinese, Aztec, or Canadian—have collectively shared the imbalance of being trapped in the mind and expelled from the garden of connection and joy.

These problem solvers, victors, and sociopaths created the textbook history most of us learned in school. It is essentially the same story told over and over again: people struggle to survive, usually pitted one against the other. One group of people experiences *themselves* as being so separate from a neighboring group that they feel warranted to kill them. They can either take what those neighbors have or protect themselves from what their neighbors might want to take from them.

The one problem we couldn't resolve with our minds was how to go beyond our minds. We couldn't stop thinking long enough to access our hearts or our connected identity. We created more and more technology and made more and more stuff. Progress was measured in GNP and the stuff we bought and sold. We ended up creating more problems than we could resolve. We couldn't stop moving and just be still. The noise sucked the silence out of everything.

Today there are countless examples of this kind of progress all around us. We were able to think of a way to genetically modify plants so insects wouldn't eat them, but couldn't sense that those plants genetically modify us when we eat them. During World War II, we thought of a way to instantly evaporate over two hundred thousand Japanese children, women, and men with just two 10,000-pound bombs, but we did not have the human empathy to prevent us from using them.

Worldwide, we cook over fifty billion farm animals a year, while the methane from their poop cooks us.

By developing a mind-dominated world culture that is severed from its heart, we have created a nightmare scenario, a perfect storm. Multiple factors that are potentially cataclysmic in themselves can easily trigger a cascade of planet-threatening conditions: extreme climate change, overnight economic collapse, pandemic disease, nuclear war, an ever-widening gap between the rich and poor, and a world-wide water shortage, just to name a few. Any one of these could activate one or all of the others.

Being stuck in the mind with little access to the heart has its consequences, none of them pretty.

Early Bloomers

Within this historical drama of misperceived aloneness, another evolutionary process has been unfolding. During these thousands of years, small numbers of individuals around the world somehow evolved out of the dominant perception of separation, and have been able to experience themselves as *both differentiated and undifferentiated at the same time.* In evolutionary terms, they were "early bloomers." We have often referred to them as saints, sages, and teachers. They have appeared in every culture throughout history. Even though only a few are known to us today, these aware-ones have managed to radically change the world. We still call on some of them:

Jesus Christ: *A new command I give you: Love one another. As I have loved you, so you must love one another.*

Gautama Buddha: *He who experiences the unity of life sees his own Self in all beings, and all beings in his own Self, and looks on everything with an impartial eye.*

The Prophet Muhammad: *Be kind, for whenever kindness becomes part of something, it beautifies it. Whenever it is taken from something, it leaves it tarnished.*

St. Teresa of Avila: *How did those priests ever get so serious and preach all that gloom? I don't think God tickled them yet. Oh, Beloved! Hurry!*

These early bloomers went through a mystical flip of perception. We can use many different words to represent their transformed perceptual state: enlightened, reborn, One with All That Is—pick your favorite term. I call them "Heart Awakened."

Heart Awakening is an evolutionary leap in consciousness. It is not something we do or control, any more than an acorn controls its own journey from a seed to a tree. Everyone is awakening. We are just in different stages of realizing it. At some point, we all blossom into full awareness of conscious connection.

Awakening into connection and empathy alters everything! It allows us to see life as it is, rather than how we have been conditioned to think it is. This change is so vast that we don't have words to adequately convey it.

It requires a death of sorts, but what dies is suffering itself. Awakening replaces fear, self-doubt, and worry with contentment and clarity. We become more alive and vital. Without fear jumping up and down screaming that we're going to die, we can better relax. That skinny, black-clad Reaper with a big old scythe on his shoulder is replaced with a much friendlier image. Survival ceases to be our central issue. Controlling others is replaced with a willingness to cooperate and co-create while living in harmony and integrity. We awaken to love and want most to participate in the Heart Awakening of others.

Awakening also gives us access to many inner gifts. These gifts can often seem like super-powers, but not the comic book kind that center on martial prowess to kill bad guys. Rather than giving us power *over* others, these gifts grant the power to experience ourselves *as* others.

Two Histories Merging

With these two histories—external and internal—we have reached a crossroads we've never experienced before. We're at a point in evolution where internal and external are merging dramatically. This is manifesting in two ways.

First, within external history, the mass culture has become so technologically advanced that the actions arising from its mind-trance are destroying the interconnecting systems that support life. Because many of us are not aware of our connection to the whole, we operate as if there is no interconnection. Through technology, our disconnected actions are being amplified a thousand times over and thus we're collectively upsetting the inter-connected balance of life itself. No one can actually destroy the connection of all things, but we can destroy things by acting in ignorance of this connection. The fragile balance we're upsetting is ecological as well as economic, political, and social.

Although civilizations have collapsed and disappeared before, as far as we know, they have never taken every other civilization on the planet with them. And they have never threatened to take so many other species with them as well.

We can disagree about why this collapse is happening and how it will affect us, but we can't disagree that collapse is taking place. That would be denial. Collapse is a natural outcome when a system is unsustainable. The ecological, economic, political, and social systems holding up what I call the *Culture of Separation* are simply not sustainable. These systems are already collapsing in many parts of the world. The upright domino we may see in our back yard can't assure us that the entire line of dominoes isn't falling elsewhere.

Secondly, the two histories are merging because what's happening within internal history has started to include something radically new:

Instead of a small handful of people awakening within the dominant culture, there are now millions of people awakening all at once in every part of the world. This has never happened before.

You and I are included within these millions! If you were not personally experiencing this leap of consciousness, you probably wouldn't know it is occurring. You would not be able to feel the collective change in awareness if it was not happening within you. The more we awaken, the more conscious we become of participating in the convergence of these two histories. The convergence is happening to us and through us.

This time we're the ones Heart Awakening. We don't need lofty titles, nor do we need to feel special. We aren't special, just as the Heart-Awakened-Ones in the past never considered themselves to be special. One saint expressed his ordinariness by referring to himself as "the dust of the dust under the feet of others."

Realizing that the Culture of Separation is collapsing as millions of people are awakening can give us a clear framework for what is happening every day in the world around us. It starts with the fact that many of us begin our mornings wondering what the *crisis du jour* will be. Will it be a crisis in the outer world: a deadly new virus, an earthquake, a terrorist attack? Or a personal crisis: will I lose my job, find out a family member has cancer, or learn that my partner wants to be with someone else? Whatever it is, the calamity menu is long and varied. Each event can seem unrelated to the crisis that came the day before.

By understanding that we are awakening collectively, we have access to a single context that gives all these seemingly irresolvable problems meaning and purpose. By understanding the context, we're better able to accept and do whatever is needed, knowing that these events will, in all likelihood, continue. We're not shocked or victimized by them, nor do we deny their significance or difficulty. More importantly, we have a frame of reference for how we can respond to the dramatic events and dilemmas that keep occurring with greater and greater frequency.

This single context is the understanding that all personal problems such as drug addiction, obesity, depression, and dysfunctional relationships, as well as all global problems, including climate change, terrorism, economic disparity, and political tyranny, can happen only when the vast majority of people aren't yet able to access the wisdom and power of their awakened hearts.

The world we create, personally and collectively, perfectly reflects the beliefs, awareness, and perceptions we have about our world. The ways we mate, raise our children, grow our food, wage war, play, do business, govern ourselves, and relate to nature are all governed by how intrinsically connected we feel to life and to our world.

Some people can easily and understandably scoff at the idea that the solution to climate change and all our other major global issues is an increase of awareness and love. They may sarcastically say, "Yeah right! We just need enough people to open their hearts, then, poof, all our problems go away!" Yet this is exactly how it goes. Several million fully Heart-Awakened people might easily transform the planet and resolve the problems we face. It took just a few saints to change the world in the past. Think of what several million saints could do today. Collective awakening will bring us opportunities and possibilities we can hardly comprehend. Imagine a majority of human beings living open-heartedly with each other and attuned to life.

This isn't a utopian dream. It's a collective imperative.

The merger of our two histories will produce an altogether new history of how we deal with the collapse of the Culture of Separation and, simultaneously, create the Culture of Connection. How this new story unfolds in the next fifteen to forty years—which is within most of our lifetimes, or at least the lifetimes of our children—will determine how life on this planet unfolds during the next several centuries.

High Overhead

Those two red tail hawks
Circling high overhead
Floating around and around
With such grace
Seem to know exactly
What they're doing.

Don't believe this for a moment.

They're actually drunk
Totally drunk on love
Love for each other
In love with Love itself.
They couldn't fly in a straight line
Even if they wanted to.

Rabbits, run free!
Field mice, keep playing!
Scampering squirrels, relax.
They're not hungry for you.
They're not even looking down!
Their eyes are locked on one another
Their wings on fire
Their bird-hearts beating wildly.

This is hawk foreplay you're watching.

Actually
Love does this to most birds.
It makes them feather-hot and happy-high.

Once you know what's really going on up there
You'll see drunk birds
Flying around
Everywhere.

3

THE FIVE WAYS
OF BEING

My Circle Discovery

After my three-day initiation into connected-awareness at the age of twenty-one, I continued to explore Heart Awakening. Over the years, I periodically had many heart-opening experiences. Eventually, I reached a point where chasing the experience—or the ecstasy of the experience— was replaced with a simple desire to be more open-hearted. I wanted to be kinder. I wanted to be more attentive to what was happening in the moment. I wanted to be more grateful and more in wonder. I wanted to be closer to nature and to be more socially active. I wanted to be a better mate, parent, grandfather, and friend.

In 1985, my trek into the world of deeper heart awareness brought me to circle work. In circle work, people simply sit together—in a circle, as you might have guessed—with the common intention of being fully present and attentive to one another. There is no belief required in order to be in the circle, no set of practices to follow and no complex format. It's a come-as-you-are party in which we practice empathic listening, honest communication, and just "being ourselves."

For me, discovering circle was another form of coming home. How we were with one another in circle made sense to me. I could relax. I also knew I had found my life's work. I began studying group dynamics and began learning how to facilitate circles that could support what I was most interested in: evolutionary Heart Awakening and creating conscious community.

I first began studying circle dynamics in Toronto with Ross Laing, an amazing group dynamics pioneer. After several years of working with Ross, I began forming and facilitating circles on my own. I became an independent circle facilitator. I started men's circles, family circles, business circles, church circles, and even women's circles.

Being in so many circles allowed me to be with other people who were exploring personal transformation. I had a unique opportunity to witness and learn from my direct involvement with their explorations, while continuing to learn from my own. These circles became my class-room, laboratory, and ongoing social experiment for exploring Heart Awakening and community building.

Within circle, there wasn't a guru or enlightened teacher to direct anyone. There was no prescriptive lifestyle to follow. Beliefs about this or that only got in the way of following inner guidance. And instead of transcending the everyday issues of life, we were there to face them. We dealt with the kinds of questions that make life so rich and difficult: how to make our marriages work, how to be good parents, or how to generate income without selling our creative selves short. Many of us were dealing with post-traumatic stress—not the kind that came from being in war, but the kind that came from growing up in unsafe, dysfunctional families. We grappled with how to respond to climate change, terrorism, ridiculous politics, broken school systems, funda-mentalist religions, racism, and a greed-based economy. There was the challenge of dealing with personal addiction—not just the well-known addictions to alcohol and drugs, but the subtler addictions to work, sex, over-consumption, and over-thinking.

We found it didn't work to overlay these issues with chants, happy thoughts, or some kind of certainty that we were on the right path. Circles don't have paths going through them. Everyone simply has an open invitation to find out what they are truly feeling and wanting in the moment.

I learned a great deal about human behavior and group dynamics from being in so many circles. I began to understand how groups actually work. I learned why some friendships, families, and organizations function well and why others don't. I tracked the kinds of agreements we can make with one another to ensure that being together is enjoyable and productive. I learned how to deal with conflict and differences so that these things bring people closer together rather than sucking the life out of their relationships.

Most importantly, I began to see how to intentionally organize groups so that people are personally transformed by being in them. To me, exploring the vast potential in how we connect and create together within all the social groups we are part of is an entirely new frontier.

I was well aware that, even though we spend most of our daily lives within some kind of group or another, our culture teaches almost nothing about how our groups can function more effectively and connectively. This omission helps feed the fallacy that we are completely alone even while we are in families, partnerships, schools, jobs, grocery store lines, sports teams, political parties, friendships, gangs, religious organizations, book clubs, neighborhoods, apartment buildings, towns, nations, birthday parties, relationships, and service organizations, just to name a few.

I saw that while parents teach their children all kinds of things, no one teaches parents how to make the family a functional, happy, loving, social organism. I've seen how schools offer classes in many subjects, while their teachers may not know how to make each class an integrated unit where everyone in it feels connected with and supported by one another.

When my daughter was in medical school, I saw how aspiring doctors spend thousands of hours learning about their patients' bodies, but are taught almost nothing about how to be with the patients them-selves. That would be funny if it didn't have such vast implications for our collective health.

While in couples' circles, I watched how most committed relation-ships were driven by each partner's hidden fear of intimacy. Sitting in circle offered those willing couples a safe environment to explore the fears they were hiding from themselves and their partners. As they did this, other couples gained courage to follow. Trust grew and people connected more deeply with their mates and with everyone else in the circle.

In this way, I was discovering how community is born. I was learn-ing group anatomy and how a group functions as a living entity. As a professional facilitator, I couldn't help but notice that the fears I saw other circle members dealing with were the same fears I had. Rather than hiding behind my role as facilitator, I chose to do my own inner work along with everyone else. I simply had to recognize when the circle had become strong enough to allow me to take on this dual role. It was a humbling and important step for me. My facilitating and fully participating at the same time inspired circle members to be more authentic themselves. The circle became a safe place for all of us to look at things the mass culture is committed to keeping at bay.

While I learned a lot about how to facilitate circles through trial and error, it wasn't trial and error that taught me the most. There was an entirely new kind of teaching process in play. It was about accessing the collective wisdom of the circle itself.

We create an energetic field of intelligence simply by being together within any group. This field is made up of the combined emotions, thoughts, energies, histories, intelligence, weaknesses, and love of each person in the circle. As I sat in as several circles a day, year after year, I slowly learned how to read this energy field. I learned how it weakened when we were not being honest with each other, and how it strengthened whenever someone faced something he or she was terrified to face. This ever-changing field became my most trusted teacher.

The circle is the teacher. It never runs out of things to teach me, as long as I am willing to let go of what I think I already know.

It was by being in circle that I recognized The Five Ways of Being.

The Five Ways of Being

While sitting in circles year after year, I kept seeing that there are specific, elemental life skills that must be incorporated into everyday life in order for our hearts to awaken. These skills can also be thought of as self-inquiries, or ongoing questions, or as ways of being, that precede and continue beyond the initiation of having an awakening experience such as I had. They are practices we cultivate, investigate, and hold in our awareness. Heather Williams, one of the primary encouragers of this book, named them "The Five Ways of Being."

The Five Ways of Being provide a practical way of describing and approaching what Heart Awakening actually is. They cut across all religious and spiritual traditions. They go beyond belief. They apply to all people regardless of age, gender, nationality, or race. These practices don't rely on beautiful but nebulous concepts such as love, forgiveness, wonder, or surrender. They are far more down to earth than that. They involve no techniques or practices that promise that you will wake up in seven easy steps if you buy my formula to do so. This framework for personal transformation and inner study can't be trademarked or turned into something that I or anyone else can own. It's simply an accurate, useful way of making sense out of the countless different and often opposing teachings, processes, lifestyles, values, and ideas available within today's explosion of spiritual technology—a technology spreading at lightning speed through the Internet, and through the inner-net of our collective consciousness.

In a truly functional, heart-centered world, these inquiries or practices are what mothers and fathers would model for their children.

As we continue to evolve into Heart Culture, they will be taught and encouraged in schools from the first day of kindergarten through college graduation. They'll form the foundation for all political platforms and governmental organization. They are what saints, sages, and teachers throughout time have taught, long before their teachings were concretized into belief systems, moral codes, and instruments of institutional control. They create what my friend Franca Baroni, author of *Cor Publicum,* calls the "Public Heart."

Here is the synopsis of these Five Ways of Being or five ongoing inquiries:

- Being Clear: What is my life purpose? How does what I do in everyday life support my purpose?

- Being Present: How do I stop my constant thinking and come into stillness?

- Being Real: What am I feeling emotionally in this moment?

- Being Connected: Am I experiencing love and connection right now?

- Being Heart-Directed: Am I following what I truly want, or what I'm conditioned to want?

For me, Heart Awakening is accepting the ongoing invitation to become Clear, Present, Real, Connected, and Heart-Directed in any given moment. No one can tell us *how* to engage in these Ways of Being or self-reflective inquiries, yet, at some point, each of us must engage in them if we want to evolve into deeper awareness.

There is a similarity with these inquiries to playing a sport like basketball. If we want to play the game, we must engage in passing the ball, running up and down the court, dribbling, shooting, rebounding, and defending. We have to cultivate these elements and bring them into the game because that's what the game is. There's no final mastery of it. We just keep playing and improving as we play. The more we develop our play, the more the possibilities for enjoying it increase.

While Heart Awakening is not about *doing* practices like dribbling or shooting, there is spiritual practice involved. Inquiry into and cultivation of the Five Ways of Being are required for becoming more aware and heart-present. We must explore our purpose, quiet our minds, fully feel our emotions, come into connected love, and follow what we truly want.

These specific inquiries work synergistically with one another. One inquiry without the other doesn't work. They all combine and build on one another.

How we work with these elements is up to us. There is no "one way" for any of it, and it doesn't work if we try to prescribe or project what works for us onto somebody else. These inquiries must happen on our terms, be pursued in our own way and in our own time. The Five Ways of Being can serve as a valuable map to help us determine where we want to go, by giving us more traveling options. As a framework for awakening, it never runs out of room. It remains as fresh as the moment of Now. It's powerful because it takes us out of linear time and into the experience of Now.

The Five Ways of Being are not new. I have simply identified them. *I am not saying they are the only ways of being, just that these five ways are elemental.* You will recognize—and hopefully deem obvious—what you read about them in the next five chapters.

Everything starts with Being Clear...

A Question for You

From you
A poem is demanded
Or a song from your soul
Or a dangerous work of art.

Do it
Or be assigned
To a life as a scribe
In a court-room empty.

Will your poem
Be fire filled
Sanitized
Or never consigned to ink?

Will your song
Be sung by one million
By one
Or by none at all?

Will your art
Be timeless and powerful
Praised by liars
Or noticed by no one?

It's your poem
Your song
Your art
Your life and daily decision.

What will it be?

4

BEING CLEAR
What Is My Purpose?

Train Ride

Imagine waking up one morning and, instead of finding yourself in your own bed in your own house, you are on a passenger train speeding across a landscape you don't recognize. On the train with you are thousands of other passengers. You don't know how you got on the train, where it's going, or who these fellow passengers are. It's not possible to get off the train because there are no stops, and to jump off is certain death.

As you begin to mingle with the other passengers, you discover something additionally strange about this train ride. When you ask your fellow passengers why they're on the train and where it's going, they either ignore you or tell you they're too busy to answer such frivolous questions. They avoid you if you continue to ask them. Then someone hands you a mop and says, "It's your job to clean the train floors."

As the train speeds down the tracks, your urgency to find out why you're on it, how you got there, and where it's taking you increases even more, though no one else on the train seems to care. Your primary question isn't "Where's the mop bucket and what's for lunch?" Instead, it's "For God's sake, what is happening here?" Even with no response from the others, these questions remain in the foreground of your mind while you go about mopping floors and eating lunch.

Let's complicate the situation a little further. Imagine that when you first woke up on the train, you also discovered that your gender had changed and so had your age. You are still very much you. But now, in addition to the questions of how you got here and where you're going, there is the even deeper question: "Who am I?" With a completely different body, your identity itself is in question.

As you spend more time on the train, you notice that it's hierarchically organized around merit and privilege, each rider pitted against the others in a quest to have a more comfortable trip. Some train cars are organized so that members of their particular car have more privileges than the passengers in the other cars. Whatever the arrangement, it's still about improving the ride rather than exploring its purpose and destination.

The more you experience the train, the crazier it seems. But it's not just the ride itself that's crazy. It's that no one seems to question the purpose of the train ride, or where the train is going.

Then you think the craziest thought of all: "Maybe I'm the one who's crazy for wanting to know its purpose and destination!"

Train Ride Story Reflections

The central difference between this train ride and the ride we're all on in life is that we didn't suddenly wake up on a train in a world that is totally foreign to us. We were born on the train! All the other passengers were born on it, too. Most people don't remember ever being off the train. From day one, they've only known the mop and the meal. They've been conditioned to ignore the most basic questions in life: Who am I? What is my purpose? Where am I going? How did I get here? When and where does this ride end?

Being Clear about purpose is finding the urgency within us to answer these basic questions while living in a culture that doesn't support these inquiries. Rather than supporting us in finding out where we're going, it supports us in having a better train ride—getting a better job on the train and traveling in the more exclusive cars.

Difficulties of Being Clear in a Confused Culture

In general, our mass culture normalizes our having little interest in knowing our life purpose or knowing who we are. It not only doesn't support us in exploring these questions, it holds the questions themselves to be either unimportant or unanswerable, or that they can only be answered through religion or philosophy. As a mass culture, it's as if we say together, unconsciously, "Let's all agree that we won't get too serious about asking why we're here and I'll pretend I know who I am, if you pretend as well." We sometimes even agree that these questions are counter-productive and frivolous, that they take us away from what's really important in life, like getting things done.

When enough people conspire over many generations to make these kinds of unconscious agreements, not knowing our purpose or who we are turns into a private problem that we struggle with on our own. Without social support, we can unconsciously think that we're the only ones with this issue. It can turn into a personal shortcoming that we use to negatively judge ourselves. It's not a personal problem. It's a systemic problem within the mass culture. The culture overtly discourages us from inquiring, without anyone ever verifying the reality of this suppression.

There are many fascinating ways in which the culture discourages self-reflection. First, it's simply a matter of numbers; the vast majority of people in the culture stay away from self-inquiry. So when you see thousands of people gathered in a sports arena going absolutely nuts about whether the ball crosses the goal line or goes into a net, you may think you're nuts because you couldn't care less where the damn ball goes. You have more important things on your mind, like finding out what planet you're on where everyone gets hysterical over seemingly nothing. It's truly confusing to the contemplative ones who can't normalize not knowing who they are.

More alarmingly, it's not just that the majority of people avoid self-reflection; it's that people in positions of power avoid it. Most education officials make little room for self-reflection in schools and thus determine what millions of students are *not* taught. They simply leave self-knowledge out of the curriculum. In government, self-reflecting candidates are seldom elected to office. The ones who are elected end up working as adversaries rather than cooperatively. In faith communities, religious leaders teaching church doctrine rise in the ranks ahead of those who encourage believers to question or explore their beliefs. In mass communication, media moguls, like little foxes, trick millions of viewers into swallowing increasingly absurd levels of distraction, noise, and disinformation, making self-reflection harder to hold.

In the mass culture of confusion, those who *are* deeply committed to self-inquiry and clarity of purpose generally receive little access to the public microphone. Those seeking money, power, and prestige are rewarded with what they seek, while people seeking clarity of purpose—who are therefore not as interested in what the rest of the culture so highly values—are marginalized and quietly ignored. While there are exceptions, this is still the general rule.

Another way mass culture discourages self-inquiry is to represent the search for purpose and identity as a purely intellectual endeavor. The problem here is that intellectually based inquiry will often only produce mental answers. Mental answers either blink then disappear, or they turn into dogmatic certainty. We can dry up the whole, rich, juicy process of inquiry by turning it into something philosophical.

By confusing intellectual thought with spiritual realization, I mistake my bathtub for the ocean.

Religion can also play a powerful role in discouraging self-inquiry. Religious institutions often provide people with a pre-packaged, externalized answer to what each person's purpose should be, before he or she has a chance to find answers on their own. The church often tells its congregants what they need to believe about purpose and identity in order to join the church. They will say our purpose is to accept Jesus, or that purpose can only be known through reading the Holy Koran. The irony, of course, is that Jesus and Muhammad came into wisdom through direct experience and self-reflection, rather than through following the established temple priests or the old tribal beliefs.

By *not* experiencing identity and deeper purpose, millions of people inevitably get caught in trivial pursuits that have no distinct purpose. Days and weeks turn into years in which the main focus in life is making the body beautiful, earning and spending lots of money, playing computer games, chasing after power and success, collecting comic books or stamps, or getting high on one thing or another. The hidden purpose of following these trivial pursuits is seeking pleasure and avoiding pain, with death serving as the ultimate pain to avoid.

Waking up in a narcoleptic culture is not an easy thing to do. The culture creates a hysterically loud, interfering noise that makes it extremely difficult to listen to and hold on to the quiet needed for self-reflection. A collective din is created by family members, friends, teachers, business owners, politicians, media and entertainment personalities, doctors, and soldiers who all stay busy and in constant motion, afraid to sit still quietly. There is no judgment in this. It's just loud, like the biker who needs the roar of a Harley-Davidson between his or her legs to feel empowered. That bike is designed to make noise, like the mass culture that produced it.

Being Clear

My inquiries into my purpose and identity are ultimately led by one thing: my longing to know who I am and what this life is for. No one can teach me *how* to inquire. There's no how-to involved. There are no maps, steps, processes, systems, or models needed. Dogma doesn't count here. No one can tell me who I am or why I'm here. But I can be encouraged to inquire. We don't teach a child to crawl and walk. We only smile and cheer them on as they do. Inquiring into why we are here and who we are is natural. We don't need anyone to tell us what the answer is. We need people, relationships, and social institutions to cheer us on as we come across our longing to know.

Our inquiry into purpose is a living question, a *lived-into* question. It's ongoing. It is never settled once and for all. Instead, the inquiry itself becomes a navigational tool to find inner direction. For these questions to take hold, they must become our most valued companions, our highest priority, and our deepest desire in life.

Sustaining this inquiry into purpose in everyday life is not easy. If I'm truly searching for my purpose, I may wake up in the middle of the night sweating for an answer. My search may create havoc in my neat and tidy life. If my inquiry doesn't feel dangerous, or if it doesn't enlist my total attention, or if it doesn't disturb at least some of my friends and family members, then it's not much of an inquiry at all. True inquiry into purpose and identity brings up whatever has been in the way, as I get closer to an answer. That's why it's a process. The inquiry itself measures my willingness to face fear, because it's only fear that keeps me away from the answers I seek.

There's good news in this sweat version of inquiry, rather than in the Hallmark greeting card version. I don't have to make how I deal with this question conform to anything or anyone outside of myself. There is no box the inquiry has to fit into. There are no boundaries. The inquiry takes me where *it* goes rather than where *I think* it should go.

Even though self-reflection doesn't fit into the category of something I *do*, like walking the dog or cooking a meal, it's still possible to describe what it looks and feels like. For me, it starts with a basic insight: the realization that I don't know something that seems obvious I *should* know. It's like a stranger walking up to me on the street and handing me $10,000. My first response wouldn't be to say, "Oh, $10,000! This is for me? Thank you very much!" as I head off to the bank. I would want to know what I should know: "Ah, excuse me. Why are you giving me this money?" We've been given life. At some point, I get to realize that I don't know why it has been given to me and, thus, finding out becomes something I need to know.

Do I sit with this inquiry ten minutes a day? Do I go into the desert and stay until I know? Do I ask it once and, not finding an answer, say it's unanswerable and go back to the mop and the meal? Regardless of how I go about answering these questions, my overall intent is to carry the inquiry within me wherever I go. I weave it into my awareness. Like a fire, I tend to it until it's strong enough to throw light onto the answers.

How *do* I make something a priority in my life? By making it a priority. Finding out how to prioritize this question is part of the inquiry. I hold the question until it becomes blended into my way of being in life.

The most important part of self-inquiry into purpose and identity is, for me, remembering that I require this inquiry in order to be sane. Not knowing who I am or what I am doing in life is a form of insanity, an insanity normalized by our mass culture.

Ongoing inquiry into purpose doesn't mean I'm constantly thinking to myself, "What's-my-purpose-what's-my-purpose?" This would be an inquiry of the mind. When I inquire through an intuitive place below my constant thinking, it becomes something else.

I start with the understanding that whatever I do from moment to moment comes with a subtle, inner sensation or feeling. What I'm doing may feel good, true, real, pleasurable, light, or joyful. Or, what

I'm doing may feel jangled, pointless, off-centered, shameful, slippery, disturbing, or fear-laced. This requires that I develop an awareness of these subtle feelings as I go about my day. It's a practice of first feeling, and then identifying, what I feel. Then, it's about aligning my thoughts and actions with what feels right and letting go of thoughts and actions that don't.

Following these subtle signals is what gives me internal direction, rather than my being dependent on external rules or authorities. It's experiential, heart-felt direction, rather than mental, morality-based or belief-based direction. Being externally driven leads to increased mental activity in the form of second-guessing, doubts, or strategizing the next move. Being internally led leads to sure-footedness and ease.

And again, my answers must come through experiential insight, rather than through my intellect. For example, I may sincerely ask myself, "What is my purpose?" In my initial inquiry, perhaps I get an instant mental answer, such as, "Ah, to serve humanity! Of course! I'm here to serve humanity!" I get all excited by the insight and want to go out and serve humanity. Then my cell phone rings; I forget my purpose, and I'm back to life as usual, serving no one in particular. The insight vanishes until I inquire again later.

Even when I do get really good altruistic answers from my mind, they typically have a shelf life of only ten to twelve seconds. Then they disappear. With this fruit-fly kind of staying power, I have to keep finding intellectual answers over and over again. Intellectual answers never hold.

Initially, my own mental chatter and my inability to focus on a question may frustrate me. But frustration is an important part of inquiry. Staying with the inquiry, rather than ending it, can lead to realizing that an intelligence within me exists somewhere beyond my intellect. This somewhere is *stillness*. It's where intuition and wisdom live.

To find stillness and to drop down below my mind, my inquiry into purpose must be persistent. I'll need to quietly *demand* an answer that sticks. I won't settle for anything less than an answer that feels so right to me that I won't have to remember it. It will become part of who I am. I want real insight and realization rather than an altruistic, feel-good fix.

The purpose I find in stillness will seldom be about *doing* anything, like serving humanity, raising my children, or finding a cure for cancer. Those kinds of answers come from a tricky mind. Rather than being about *doing*, my answers will be about *being*. For example, when my answer comes from stillness, it may be the same one I got from my tricky mind—"to serve humanity." Yet this deeper answer will come with the additional insight that, to truly serve humanity, I must first open my heart. I'll recognize that serving others is a natural by-product of being more loving and kind. My purpose will then be more about opening to love than about what I do with that love. In this form of loving service, I'm not actually *doing* anything, even though I may accomplish a great deal. My actions will arise out of being fully present and openhearted, which makes whatever I do effortless. In a mystical way, I disappear as the doer, and feel as though things are done through me.

Finding the words that match your own experience of this is important. Don't settle for my words if your words are better.

Being Clear is not limited to finding clarity about the big-ticket questions of purpose and identity. It also includes Being Clear from moment to moment about my purpose for doing whatever I do. What's my purpose in working where I work? If I'm studying medicine, what is my purpose for becoming a doctor? If I'm a thief, what is my purpose in stealing? If I am going to a party, what is my purpose in being there? Being intentional in this way allows me to interweave my purpose into my daily life activities, such as raising children, being in business, or dealing with crisis.

We may think this kind of inquiry into purpose takes a great deal of time, but the inquiry itself isn't what takes time. What does take time is putting off the inquiry until another time. I may think I need more spiritual practice or stronger financial security before I self-reflect. Or I may need an external event that forces me to stop and inquire, like a serious illness or the death of someone I love. All of this may be necessary. This is what takes time.

Regardless of how consciously or unconsciously I choose to proceed with my inquiry, the inquiry is always *mine* to do with whatever I want, whenever I want. I'm always free to choose. There is no such thing as a wrong choice. Life is in full support of me inquiring under my own terms. There may be consequences that come with inquiring or not inquiring, but my freedom to choose never wavers. I'm free to question whenever and however I want.

For me, the most important thing to remember about self-reflection around purpose and identity is that it never leads to ultimate answers. It leads to ever deepening answers. That's why the inquiry must be ongoing. It takes us ever deeper into the mystery of life, rather than arriving at a fantasy place of mental certainty.

Advantages of Being Clear

People who are clear about their purpose are not better than those who are not clear. They will feel better by Being Clear, but this does not make them superior to someone who isn't as clear.

The ultimate purpose we share as human beings is related, in one way or another, to opening the heart to love.

I had a friend, Paul Moss, who died of cancer several years ago. No one would ever call Paul a spiritual or religious man. He was crusty, skeptical, and tremendously kind to everyone. Two days before his passing, he smiled and whispered into the ear of Sarah, another friend, sitting by his bed.

"Hey, Sarah," he said.

"Yeah, Paul?" she said.

"I have seen what's on the other side."

"What is it, Paul?"

"Love! It's all love."

It turns out love is what's on *this* side as well.

Saying we all share the same purpose of opening the heart doesn't contradict the fact that no one can tell us what our purpose is. The reason this isn't contradictory is that, for the term *opening the heart* to have any meaning, it must come with the direct experience of heart opening. Paul Moss can tell us that love is on the other side because he was experiencing it, not because he believed it. What's true is true, whether we believe it or not. It's like gravity. Our minds have no say in the matter.

Saints and sages in every culture throughout time have all said the same things about love and purpose. But knowing this as a mental idea and experiencing it from moment to moment can be two very different things. One's the menu and the other is the meal.

Being Clear is the First Way of Being. In order to be clear, we also must climb into the Second Way of Being: Being Present. These two friends go everywhere together.

Let's go there next.

Like a Cat

Like a cat, be still
Until one-pointedness
Directs the pounce.
Patience pays.

Hold the brush high
Until the heart
Moves the hand.
This is art.

Judge not at all
Until the facts
Speak first.
Act only then.

This is all written.

5

BEING PRESENT

Can I Quiet My Mind
And Be Still?

Big Sister

The classic sci-fi thriller *Blade Runner* presents a futuristic urban setting in which those in power broadcast a calm Big Sister voice over the entire city, telling people whatever the government wants them to hear. It sounds like that recorded voice at the airport that keeps reminding us to report any unattended bags to the authorities. Imagine you live in a culture like this, in which the powers that be not only broadcast their commands every ten minutes like at the airport, but every moment of every day.

This voice invades you everywhere you are: at work, at sporting events, when you are out for a meal, or back in your home. Not only does this voice tell you things the powers want you to know, but it also tells you what they want you to do and what they forbid you to do. It tells you what to believe and which people are safe or dangerous. It tells you what to buy, what movies to see, what countries to hate.

This ever-present voice can also get quite personal. It tells you what's beautiful, what's ugly, what's real, and what's false. It dictates what you should do with your life and informs you of the penalties for not doing so. The worst part about this voice is that you can't shut the damn thing off. It keeps broadcasting anything it wants directly into your consciousness, so that you hear it while making love, eating pizza, or combing your hair.

This Big Sister voice has another endearing trick that really messes with your mind. She broadcasts nonsense—trivial things, things that don't make sense and have no meaning. She may sound like this: "You are a bad person and the stock prices fell two hundred points after news that the Federal Reserve Chairman was sick so there is a forty percent chance of showers that will increase when your mail delivery stops because your partner is looking a little tired today. And by the way, sometimes you are a great person and God loves you but watch out for body odor and bad breath."

Imagine how really obnoxious and disruptive this could be when you are at a concert, walking in the woods, or doing yoga. It continues to yap its ever-present news, commands, nonsense, and alerts. Perhaps more importantly, imagine how that voice could get in the way when you want to concentrate on something that's really important to you, like taking an exam, closing a sale, or grieving the loss of someone you love.

Big Sister Story Reflections

As you may have guessed, the story of this Big Sister broadcasting system is actually about the ongoing chatter in our heads. While the mass culture does broadcast its own version of Big Sister, it pales in comparison to our own constant thinking, our internal critic, and our fountain of nonsense and opinionated thought.

It's easy for me to think the man walking down the street talking wildly to no one in particular is crazy. It's a little harder to catch that that's how *I* am when I can't stop thinking, when I can't seem to end the ongoing conversation I'm having with myself in my head. Internally, I can be spewing thoughts, rants, raves, judgments, and nonsense that rivals any street talker. But on the outside, I'm polite, polished, and sane. No one can hear the noise in my head.

Sometimes, when I try to stop thinking, I find that my mind has a mind of its own. Like a car kept idling all day long, I can't rest. I come into sanity when I enter stillness. I enter stillness simply by being still. I am sane when I witness my thoughts and feelings, rather than being consumed by them. I'm no longer crazy when I'm willing to find out why I am so afraid to be present.

When I stay stuck in endless thought and continuous forward motion, I suffer in many ways. Wisdom teachers have said for centuries that happy human beings are those who spend ninety percent of their time enjoying life through their senses and ten percent using their mind to solve problems and take care of business. When I mimic the vast majority of people in our culture, this ratio is reversed: ninety percent of my time is spent thinking about life and ten percent is spent feeling it. I'm too busy solving problems to actually feel the magnificence of being alive. Clear thinking is essential; over-thinking is a curse.

The biggest disadvantage of being mind-centered is that I don't feel the people I'm with. I'm too busy coating them with my silent mental commentary to enjoy them as they are. When I'm constantly talking to myself, I'm not present. My children hate this. All they want is my presence. My partner is the first to point out my lack of presence. She didn't sign up for an absentee mate—a man who can't stop and be still with her.

Without presence, friendships hollow out. Work becomes a grind. Over-thinking leaves little room for my clear thoughts to surface. Too much busyness keeps me from taking care of business. The wheat gets lost in the chaff.

Constant thought and busyness make it hard for me to celebrate anything—a birthday, a holiday, a success, or an anniversary. They also make it difficult to grieve. In fact, I can think myself out of feeling any emotions, be they joyful or painful, and thus lose the encoded intelligence within them. Without emotional intelligence, when I come to a choice, my gut won't tell me which way to turn. My default response to everything will be rational. It's like forever walking in the color grey.

Difficulties of Being Present in a Busy Culture

Being caught in relentless thought and busyness is often unbearable. It creates an unsustainable pressure on my nervous system that, at some point, must be released. When I don't release this pressure by simply being still, I must rely on something outside of stillness if I want to relax. Anything will do: television, texting, or talking too much. There's always sports, sex, or drugs of every kind. Over-eating is reliable as well. But the strangest thing of all is becoming even busier than I was before.

A mass culture steeped in busyness will sponsor us in any addiction we want.

Constant thinking is one thing, but constant self-destructive thinking is another. Thoughts can be so infused with dark shadows and mental shards that a person can think it's time to end it all. This thought can be acted out in the moment or played out in installments over time. Anyone can become dangerous to themselves and others when they mistake their dark thoughts for reality. The rope in the road can be mistaken for a snake that's ready to strike.

If I can't stop thinking, I won't be able to feel who I am nor know my purpose. I won't feel embodied. I will do things that make absolutely no sense because those things won't be tied to my deeper purpose.

Being Present in our Culture of Separation isn't easy. Our mass culture is noisy—really, really noisy. Being Present and still doesn't *require* quiet spaces or the silence of nature, but these environments do help. Being with people who love stillness also helps. The difficulty of being still becomes harder yet when being with others increases the noise in our heads, rather than helping us reduce it. You know this if you've ever walked in nature with someone who loves words more than the woods.

Our mass culture has a noisy Saturday night flavor to it. I'm not complaining. I'm just saying it can be challenging to be present when the Tower of Babel has an endless party going on.

The speed at which everything is moving in our electronic culture is in direct opposition to the pace of life that supports being still. In many ways, we are moving a hundred times faster than the culture of a hundred years ago. We have few teachers or gurus who have grappled with this speed because no other culture in the history of the world has ever moved this fast. Not even close.

Being Present and being still are not taught in school. By leaving it off the curriculum, the message is delivered that presence is not important in life. In our mass-culture education, we are trained to think but never taught how to stop thinking. When school budgets are cut, the first things to go are the classes like music, sports, and art, where being able to feel life is more important than thinking about it. Metaphorically, children come out with lopsided brains when they're forced to think too much; their left hemispheres seem much bigger than their right.

In general, there is no collective cultural agreement that Being Present is important. Without it, little attention is paid to how we deal with the pressures that come with this ever-increasing speed. It's just busyness as usual, as if life today is the same as it was in the 1920's. We don't even have vocabulary or reference points to talk about presence, or the need for it.

Schools teach constant thinking. Businesses insist on it. Parents are caught in it, and the media drives it.

We don't know how all of this is affecting our quality of life, our sense of self, our general health, or our ability to connect with others. Although this pressure is brand new to us, we pretend it's normal. We're like the frog being incrementally cooked in a kettle without being aware things are heating up. It's a whole new kind of crazy.

This extreme pressure is exacerbated by seeing life-and-death problems all around us without having any power to resolve them: mass killings, monster weather change, species decimation, body-eating viruses, and savage wars without visible combatants. The intellect is for solving problems, so when I am electronically exposed to so many problems in the world, my mind stays busy—consciously or not—looking for solutions for things I cannot solve. This creates a generalized frustration and sense of impotence. Even though the pressure of this overexposure is new, it has already been normalized by the mass culture. No one is talking about it. It's silent insanity.

The personal demands on our time and energy are expanding exponentially each year. As a householder, I need to generate income, parent my children, maintain my partnership, keep friendships alive, and manage the houseful of stuff I accumulate over time. In times past, the few people who were sincere about Being Present found their way to the empty desert, the quiet monastery, or Walden Pond. They could stay for a year or two. That's not realistic for most of us now. As householders, we have to feed the cat at home and feed the boss at work. It's challenging.

The most difficult part of quieting my mind is what happens when I first try to be still. Feelings start to arise—feelings I have avoided by staying in constant thought. The more present and still I am, the more I feel life within and around me. This includes feeling trauma I carry with me from the past. Stillness creates space for the memories of this trauma to surface. When we experience trauma that's too difficult to feel at the time it's occurring, we have an amazing ability to put our painful emotions into deep freeze. Being still thaws these feelings. It brings them out of the subconscious mind into consciousness. Once unfrozen, they can feel as new as the day they originally occurred. We'll experience the old trauma as if it's happening in present tense. Feeling these stored emotions as they arise out of seemingly nowhere can be terrifying. It can also be confusing, especially if I think being still will automatically bring me peace, love, and bliss rather than confusion, anxiety, and terror. There are some pretty mean guard dogs stationed at the gates of stillness.

Being Present and still also means taking an honest look at my own social conditioning: my looped thoughts, parental implants, and automatic responses that I began accumulating in childhood. All these things begin to surface the moment I'm willing to be still. This isn't fun. Facing snarling dogs seldom is. Constant thinking turns out to be a cover for what I'm afraid to feel. It insures the truth is out of view. It can be tempting to keep it that way.

In mass culture's spiritual marketplace, where all things spiritual are bought and sold, it's much more profitable to sell meditation practices than it is to simply encourage someone to sit still and feel into whatever they are feeling in that moment. Meditation can be turned into a tangible product—a technology, a *how-to*, or a standardized procedure that can be packaged and marketed. It is a cause-and-effect arrangement the seller makes with the buyer. The seller pretends to have something that will produce the perfect outcome that someone else desires. The seller just has to convince the buyer of this and the sale is made. We can't really sell stillness. It makes a poor commodity because anyone can come into it, anywhere, anytime. It's an inquiry, instead of something we do. "Am I feeling present right now? If not, do I really want to pause and be still?"

This can be difficult for any of us raised in a culture where doing something is the answer to everything. We can become steady consumers of the latest and greatest self-help ploy. Our minds can be confused by the thought of doing nothing, especially when it means not *doing* yoga or *practicing* meditation.

Some of the major religions in mass culture add to this confusion.

Beliefs are mental constructs. They are ultimately a collection of mental ideas or images. They may *originate* in an actual religious experience. They often do. But when the memory of these experiences and the thoughts about these experiences are stored in the mind, *rather than re-experienced in daily life*, they become just images of the original experience. They become false images: representations of the real thing rather than the real thing itself.

Idol is another name for a false image. Holding *belief* above *direct experience* is a subtle form of idol-worship. People seriously caught in fundamentalist belief systems may tell you that you're the one worshipping false idols if you prefer stillness and presence over their beliefs. This is not only confusing, but can also be downright dangerous. If you don't agree with their beliefs or false idols, you may be threatened with eternal damnation or get your head chopped off.

Being Present

I often experience how my own beliefs get in the way of stillness. For example, when I'm still, I may access wonder and see the perfection of life. It may then be easy for me to create the belief that life is perfect, based upon my momentary experience of perfection. Then when life brings its inevitable challenges my way, instead of *feeling* the pain or the complexity of what I'm experiencing, I may be tempted to bypass what I'm feeling by *thinking*, "Life is perfect!" In doing so, I shellac over what I'm feeling with a belief about perfection. Sticky stuff.

If I were to carry this to an extreme, I might be tempted to start *The Church of Life Is Perfect*. I'd start preaching to everyone my message that life is oh so perfect even when I'm not directly experiencing it. All of this would take me away from simply being present. I'd stay busy in my new role as the founder of *The Church of Life Is Perfect*. Hopefully, sanity would prevail. I'd come back to Being Present and eventually perceiving perfection again. My need to start a church would end before

I'm crazy enough to do so.

Stillness requires letting go of beliefs, as beliefs are part of constant thinking. Sorting this out can be difficult, especially when the mass culture derives much of its power and legitimacy by maintaining certain beliefs. In most nations, aligning with the dominant national beliefs is a requirement for rising to power. If you are in a Christian nation, you must believe what Christians believe. Likewise in a Muslim nation or a Hindu nation. Again, there is no blame here.

The reliance on belief rather than trusting our direct perception is changing. The transformation is playing out in mass culture right before our eyes. Pedophile priests and beheading Islamists are doing a good job of highlighting the limitations of belief. Still, sorting this out while living in its midst can make for a bumpy ride indeed.

To be sane, I must *experience* stillness. I must discover that I can watch my thoughts and my emotions rather than be caught up in them. This is not optional. But how I go about exploring the stillness within me is always my choice. There is no single way to experience it. There is only the way that my longing leads me. It's personal. Self-customized.

Similar to Being Clear, Being Present is a process that never reaches a final state. I am ultimately led by my own longing to be present rather than by any teachings about how to be present. It happens through experience, through trial and error, moment to moment. It's spiritual natural selection at work. There is plenty of room for dead ends and detours because it's a self-correcting process. All I need is the longing to be present and the willingness to feel whatever is happening in the moment.

For many years, I longed to find a way to be still, other than simply being still. I wanted a technique, a mantra, or a two-step boogie. The problem with techniques is that I just make them into another thing to do.

What I *can* do is inquire into what keeps me from being still. I can be willing to experience the fear and frozen feelings that come up when I am still. I can choose to ignore the thoughts that tell me to get back to busyness. My desire and willingness must be fierce enough to meet the relentless surge of my habitual thinking and my recycled emotions. I can open up my senses, slow everything down, become increasingly aware of everything around me, and attune to the people I'm with. I can organize my life around my willingness to feel life rather than just think about it. And ultimately, I can love that part of me that needs to keep thinking.

Teachers and life lessons will come to me when I hold my desire to be present. The desire is enough. It's plenty. And it must be fed with resolve—gently though, without getting too serious about it.

Paradoxically, while being still requires no technique or process, techniques and processes can be valuable, and are sometimes necessary. Meditation, yoga, chanting, many forms of prayer, feeling my breathing, dancing, playing golf, vision quests, fasting, making love, serving others, affirmations, social activism, bodywork, emotional processing, talk therapy, martial arts—all of these practices can play an important part in Being Present, as long as I don't make them an end in themselves. At some point, doing these things must give way to doing nothing.

Stillness is part of our natural state. Although I can't be more present than I already am, I can become more aware of stillness and presence, rather than covering it up with the busyness our culture promotes. My longing to be still knows the way.

Advantages of Being Present

The advantages of being still and present are many. When I'm present, I have space to hear the whisper of inner guidance so that my actions don't incur debt.

In stillness, I have greater access to the panoramic view. From this wider perspective, my options open up and I can choose with greater wisdom.

When I'm present, gratitude becomes my favorite prayer.

When I'm still, I can access moving at a particular speed in life that ends up requiring no effort or struggle. It's the sweet spot where the movement itself becomes highly pleasurable. It makes the act of walking, talking, doing the dishes, or opening a door feel really, really pleasurable. It's the same pleasure that's built into everything. I just have to be still enough to feel it.

I can easily think I'm in control of my life when my mind is telling me I am. In stillness, I'm freed from this narcissistic trance. When I'm free from it, I'm always delighted to find out that my control isn't needed. It's redundant, like thinking I have to row the Queen Mary across the ocean all by myself. When I'm still, I can feel how this majestic ocean liner is quietly smiling at my oars and my effort.

When I come into true silence, I keep discovering all over again that the silence itself is running everything. When everything quiets down, I can hear life happen.

When I'm present, I'm hurled into wonder. I wonder where all of *this* came from. I don't want answers or explanations. I want to stay in wonder. Instead of solving the Mystery, I want to swim in it. Rather than thinking something's wonderful, I want to continue experiencing the wonder of it. I want to be seized by it until I melt.

When I'm still, I have a much easier time discovering my purpose. In fact, living in stillness turns out to be a large part of my purpose. And it goes further than this. Stillness also tells me who I am: I am the stillness I seek.

Cultivating presence, I can truly serve others simply by Being Present with them. My being still calls others into their own stillness, without my having to say or do anything. In this way, I serve the culture and something greater than myself.

Gratitude often follows stillness wherever it goes. When I'm with them, I may find myself crying spontaneously or laughing for no reason at all. My own mind will give me dirty looks, saying the tears and laughter are inappropriate. But what do I care? There's just so much I'm grateful for that I can't contain it all.

All of this and much, much more comes with Being Present.

Before moving on to the Third Way of Being, do you want to be still for a moment? It's a question you can always come back to, no matter how you answer it now.

Hospital Maternity Ward

Bunch of babies screaming
In the middle of the night
All lined up in parallel fright
In their pain-glass womb
Away from the breast
They lie alone together
In a mother-less nest.

Those bunch of babies screaming
In the middle of the night
Now grown up still in parallel fright
Got to be a man
So acting the part
Making love like crazy
On an empty heart.

Into presidents and dissidents
They each buy a gun
Their women out of earshot
With their tops undone.
Never ending wars
And their no-win scripts
Are the unheard screams
From their empty, soft lips.

Crying out for milk
They milk the land.
Their tiny reach for touch
Becomes a grabbing hand.
Their cry for distant love
Echoes out past the moon
While their marriages end
In frustration-filled doom.

Bunch of babies' futures
All lined up the same
An entire life spent
Thinking they are to blame.
That pain-glass ward
Separating the head from the heart
Keeping need and fulfillment
Inch-miles apart.

Senseless separation
At the time of greatest need
The loneliness, isolation
Planted then as a seed.

Bunch of babies screaming
In the middle of the night
Separated from the others
In their parallel fright.

6

BEING REAL
What Am I Feeling Right Now?

Bobby's Dog

One late afternoon in September, Bobby witnessed his own sweet dog being run over by a car in front of his house. He'd thrown a ball for her to fetch. It went too far and rolled into the street. She ran after it. Bobby thought it was his fault that she died. All he wanted was to throw that ball over again so he could sleep with her that night.

The next morning, he felt numb and withdrawn. His mother had told him the night before to stop crying because it wasn't his fault. His father had told him that crying wasn't going to bring his dog back. The message he received from both parents was that there wasn't any point in feeling how he felt. So, when he walked into his first-grade classroom, he had already begun the process of closing down the grief he felt about his dog.

Bobby's classmates didn't notice anything different about him. Although his teacher sensed that he seemed quieter than usual, she didn't say anything to him.

As much as Bobby wanted to share what had happened, first grade went on that day as if his dog had never died, much like it did the next day and the day after that. The students worked on adding and subtracting numbers and inching their reading skills forward one letter at a time. Bobby didn't inch forward anywhere that day. He felt frozen inside. Those images of his dog running into the street wouldn't go away.

By the time Bobby was in high school, his name had shortened to Bob. He was a good football player, not a bad student, and kids liked him well enough. In the eleven years between first grade and his last day of high school, other things happened in Bob's life, as things do. His parents got divorced when he was twelve. It was hard for him, but easier than listening to them argue all the time. He broke his arm skateboarding when he was thirteen. The next year his little brother went missing for an entire day and ended up being found in a town fifteen miles away. He was alive and unhurt, thank God. The police never determined what happened, and his little brother refused to talk about it.

In his senior year, there was a terrible car accident. A group of juniors out celebrating late one night after a football game crossed that yellow line and hit a pick-up truck head on. Three of them died.

Bob and his friends talked about some of these events, but not about the divorce or the mysteriously creepy thing that happened with his brother. Only the car accident was discussed at school. A psychologist was brought in to address the whole school in the auditorium for two hours.

These were the big events in Bobby's school years, the ones he remembered but would just as soon have forgotten. Sandwiched between them were the ordinary issues that many kids have to deal with today: sorting out the sex and drug thing, balancing sports and extra-curricular activities with academics, feeling socially awkward much of the time, and being totally bored by school year after year. Most students went through similar things, so there wasn't much to talk about. Like in war where soldiers don't talk about how afraid they are: everyone's afraid and everyone knows it, so what's there to say?

Bob came into his classes each school day like he had the day before, like the year before. It was never a place to talk about what was happening in his personal life. This was the same for all his classmates, as well as for the teachers and the administrators. It was like a big wall running down the center of things separating what everyone was feeling from what they were actually talking about. School was a place to learn facts and skills, not a place to learn about feelings. Everyone knew that.

And this was quite okay with Bob. It was more than okay, because ever since his dog died, he never liked talking about that kind of stuff. What good would it do?

Bobby's Dog Story Reflections

The Culture of Separation taught me I could divide my emotions into two distinct groups: good feelings and bad feelings. I tried not to feel the bad feelings: anger, rage, jealousy, envy, grief, sadness, hopelessness, fear, terror, panic, unworthiness, guilt, lust, depression, and shame. Bad feelings were dangerous or inappropriate, so I learned to not share these with others unless they erupted out of me. As for my good feelings, they were mostly confined to just one: feeling fine. I would tell people I'm feeling fine, whether I was or not. They usually told me that they were fine too.

It's a strange thing about emotions. If I know I'm angry and tell you I'm not, then I'm not being honest with you. This can be a little confusing for you if you can see that I'm angry. Where it really gets crazy for both of us is when I don't actually know what I'm feeling—like when I'm angry but can't feel it, so I tell you I'm fine. This isn't about being honest. It's about Being Real. Do I actually *know* what I'm experiencing from moment to moment? Alternatively, do I repress what I'm really feeling because I've been conditioned to think most emotions are bad? Am I afraid to feel?

I'm Being Real whenever what I *think* I'm feeling matches what I'm actually feeling, when I don't label some emotions good and others bad, when I allow what I'm feeling to roll unimpeded through my body. When I'm cut off from what I'm feeling, I lose access to the essential information my emotions carry.

Anger tells me I need better boundaries. Fear tells me to stop every-thing and be fully present. Sadness says to pay attention to something that's ending. Grief says to deal with something that has already ended. Feeling good is a green light for moving forward. Without allowing my emotions to roll through me and harvesting the information they carry, I'm walking through life blindfolded.

When I'm cut off from emotions like grief or rage, I often close down the pleasurable feelings like joy and wonder. Feelings are strung together in a unified system, like those old Christmas tree lights, where when one light goes off, they all go off. When I'm cut off from my emotions, I end up feeling numb. But this is more than emotional numbing. *All* my senses are hooked up to that light string of emotion. When I dull my feelings, my senses are dulled right along with them. If I shut down my grief, I'll often shut down my taste buds. If I'm out of touch with anger, I'll find it more difficult to feel the touch I receive from others.

When I don't know what I'm feeling, there's less chance I'll know what other people are feeling. Being in relationship with people I can't feel doesn't usually work out very well. The relationships fill up with drama and tension.

Unfelt feelings fester. They clog my arteries. They make me afraid to dance. I walk around in life on stilts. I'm zippered shut. My nerves get pinched. When I can't access my emotions, I think and act like someone I'm not.

Unfelt feelings affect every aspect of my life. They keep recycling through me, looking for a way out, for an escape hatch or a mode of expression. This inner recycling keeps my mind spinning, as my mind and my emotions are linked together. And when I can't be still, I can't feel who I am, nor do I know what my purpose is. If I'm not real, I can't be present and clear.

To be Heart Awakened, I have to be willing to inquire into what I am feeling. I have to be real.

Difficulties of Being Real in an Image-Based Culture

Being Real with my emotions isn't easy for many reasons. Here are a few of my favorites:

As I said earlier, most *personal* problems originate inside deeper systemic *cultural* problems. For example, in Bobby's story, it's quite likely that Bobby will have difficulty sustaining close intimate relationships later in his life because of his long history of repressing his emotions. He may think he alone is responsible for his relational difficulties when, in fact, his parents, his friends, the school system, and the culture itself, all operate within this same paradigm of emotional repression. His personal problems originate from much deeper systemic problems.

The Culture of Separation is simply not organized around emotional honesty. It doesn't hold emotional intelligence as a value. This is a generalized fact, rather than a judgment. It tends to reward people who repress their feelings and penalize those who don't. Bobby still has to deal with his own repressive patterns, but part of dealing with them is understanding that they are born out of greater systemic problems. These patterns are not his fault. This distinction is often extremely difficult to decipher.

To get the flavor of how emotional intelligence is devalued, imagine you are a cabinet member attending a high-level meeting with the President of the U.S., talking about the ongoing slaughter of people by terrorists in the Middle East. What if during the meeting, you actually felt the impact of this butchery on a deep emotional level? Would there be the freedom to express your empathic pain to the others gathered around that table? Not likely. There is an unspoken rule in place that such emoting is highly inappropriate. More than likely, you would be shamed and henceforth thought of as being weak.

Yet policy made without empathy creates weak policy. For example, let's say that the slaughter in the Middle East is occurring because the terrorists can't feel the people they're killing. Cabinet members perpetuate the problem when they don't feel or won't express the horror of what they are witnessing. Therefore, policy-making stays only on a mental, thought-based level. Not able to feel the people their policy affects, they decide to send in the drones. The drones kill enemy combatants and innocent civilians, whose relatives sign up for the next suicide mission. And on and on it goes.

In the 2016 U.S. presidential campaign, one devout Christian candidate said that his answer to the mess in the Middle East was "carpet-bombing."

After taking a moment to let that sink in, let's switch over to the opposite end of the emotional spectrum: endless emotional processing. As difficulties go, this is big one. It's not as big as carpet-bombing, but it's big.

First, what do I mean by emotional processing?

As I said in the previous chapter, we have a capacity to numb and separate from our feelings. This is similar to what happens when our home electrical system becomes overloaded. If the wires can't handle the excess current, a fuse blows and shuts down the flow of electricity so that the overloaded wires don't burn down the house. In early childhood, when we experience emotional pain too great for our young nervous system to handle, we shut down our emotional system in a similar way. An emotional fuse blows. We go into shock. Because we have to keep functioning in everyday life, we store the shock from this emotional overload inside our bodies. Then, ideally, we wait until we are mature enough to better process the stored trauma. Often, the memory of the trauma itself goes into hiding along with the emotions. The accumulation of all of these stored traumas make up what Eckhart Tolle calls *the pain body*.

The pain body and the conditioned beliefs we adapt to keep the pain body from being re-activated are the primary factors that keep us from Being Real. We develop a compensatory personality built around keeping that pain in storage, out of our everyday awareness. Examples of this include being distant and aloof with others because we subconsciously remember being hurt by a caregiver. We don't want to be hurt again. Or we become aggressive with others to compensate for an earlier time when caregivers or siblings were aggressive towards us.

We adapt to early life trauma in the best way we can. We are pre-wired to do this. It helps us survive. Emotional wounding is passed on from generation to generation like a treasured family heirloom.

The cycle continues until one child in the family lineage matures into an adult who's ready to face their stored pain and hidden beliefs. That person must have the courage and the willingness to re-feel the feelings associated with the trauma and inquire into whether or not the beliefs they created around that trauma are in alignment with reality today. For example, if someone was abused as a child, that person must not only thaw out and feel the frozen feelings surrounding the abuse, but may also have to deal with the subconscious belief that he or she deserved to be abused. This requires tenacity, courage, and focus.

Intentionally bringing these stored emotions and hidden beliefs into consciousness is what I'm referring to as "processing emotions."

When buried emotions surface into consciousness for the first, second, or third time, they often come with a euphoric state. Feelings are released that have been weighing us down for what may seem like forever. We enter a state akin to being high. When more memories are accessed and released, there are more highs to be had. If we join a bunch of people processing their emotions at an emotional releasing workshop, we'll invariably end up with a big party where everyone's getting stoned on emotional releasing. Or we may prefer a private party, in which case we can find a therapist who specializes in emotional release, and party down every week for as many sessions as we can afford.

At this juncture in our newfound processing adventure, three standard difficulties arise. I speak of these difficulties from the place of having directly experienced them. When I first began facilitating circle, I was an emotional process junkie. I specialized in emotional release work.

The first difficulty is that it's easy to relate to our emotions as *things*— things we have or possess, e.g. my anger, my grief, or my shame. Given that they're negative *things*, we'll have a natural desire to be a rid of them—to clear them out—until we're completely free from them. But this doesn't work. As I said previously, emotions provide us with essential information; in fact, emotions *are* information. They are signposts that give us direction in life.

The second difficulty is related to the first. We often take on the mistaken notion that by clearing all these emotions out of us, we'll be able to maintain the euphoric state we experienced from releasing them. We can easily create an idealized version of reality in which we believe that once our emotions and old beliefs are cleared, we'll live in a euphoric, stoned-like state forever. There will be a tendency to think that this is what spiritual teachers are referring to when they talk about enlightenment or awakening. It's not. It's a trap.

The third difficulty follows on the heels of the first two. There are thousands of programs and processes available in the self-help sector of our economy that go along with this mistaken idea that emotional clearing leads to some form of enlightenment. For example, we can do Holotropic Breathwork and emotions will come up—lots of them. We can do Rational Emotive Behavior Therapy, a powerful process that promises to free us from trauma with its specialized eye movement and skull-tapping. We can fast to cleanse our emotional and physical bodies. The marketplace has the product or service for us if we're willing to buy into this idea of "getting rid of negative emotions."

The problem, of course, is that emotions are not *things*. We don't have to "process" them. Having a safe space to simply feel and express them is often essential in trauma work. Also, from my personal experience, there's great value in techniques such as Holotropic Breathwork, REBT, and fasting. However, trying to use these practices to *clear* our emotions doesn't work. Repetitive emoting can go on forever. It can also re-traumatize us by overloading our nervous systems once again.

As we stop thinking that we have to get rid of our emotions, we stop wanting to chase the high that comes with their release. We stop thinking that enlightenment is a state—something we go into and out of—rather than being reality itself.

Being Real in a mass culture that doesn't organize itself around emotional honesty is also difficult because we have so many ways to distance ourselves from what we are feeling.

I can repress my feelings: "What do you mean, I seem angry?"

I can deny what I'm obviously feeling: "*I'm* not angry, damn it!"

I can project my feelings onto others: "Why are *you* so angry?"

I can transcend my emotions: "I've outgrown anger, My Love ..."

And I can rationalize not feeling my emotions: "I don't have time to be angry!"

Being Real

I have a friend in Boulder, Colorado, named Raven Wells. While out for breakfast one morning, he showed me a personal transformation model he'd drawn up on his napkin about how we evolve as humans. I loved the model and smiled at the napkin. He said that we go through three distinct stages: child, adolescent, and adult. Because this was nothing new to me, it might have been a waste of napkin, but he went on to say that we further evolve into three more stages after becoming adults. We first become *conscious adults*. Then we mature into what he calls *conscious conduits*. And finally, if there is a finally, we become *awake beings*. He said that our mass culture doesn't recognize the existence of these three additional stages and this can be quite confusing for those people who are developing into them.

My interpretation of his napkin wisdom fits perfectly into what I'm saying about Being Real. As I move from being an adult into being a *conscious adult*, I become aware that, even though I am chronologically an adult, I often feel quite young and immature, not to mention neurotic at times. I also start noticing how crazy the culture is: we actually slaughter each other in the name of God? We eat food purposely laced with toxic chemicals? I'm feeling rage but I tell you I'm fine?

According to Raven, we move from being an adult to being a *conscious adult* when we wake up on that speeding train and realize we don't have a clue who we are, where we are going, or with whom we are traveling.

As a *conscious adult*, we start the process of self-inquiry. We have to own that we're a bit crazy, without being self-critical about it: it's a fact, not a judgment. Being Real about this allows us to explore our beliefs, repressed feelings, and the habits that make us neurotic. This *conscious adult* stage can go on for months, which is usually not the case, or for years, which usually is the case. Our commitment to Being Real has much to do with our willingness to spend the necessary time in this *conscious adult* developmental stage. It often isn't much fun.

Then we evolve into what Raven calls the *conscious conduit* stage. In this stage, we weave in and out of our own craziness. We have life-changing insights into who we are and what our purpose is. We're present one moment and obsessed by busyness the next. We allow ourselves to feel our emotions rather than repressing them. We go in and out, in and out, for what can seem like a long, long time. We are actually learning everything we can from being both *in* and *out* (feeling connected and disconnected). That's the *conscious conduit* stage. It can be much more fun than the *conscious adult* stage when we're feeling connected, and more painful than the *conscious adult* stage when we're feeling disconnected.

And then comes the bonus prize. We can evolve into being *consciously awake. (Here comes the sun!)* Instead of going in and out of duality, confusion, and disconnection, we remain clear and present most of the time. It's not so much that we are always *in* and never *out*. It is more like the *out* is just as valuable as the *in*. We stop categorizing our feeling state and simply be with *what is*. We whisper into our own ear, "The struggle's over."

From my own experience, moving from the first three developmental stages to the next three stages involves one essential life skill: witnessing. Witnessing is being able to step outside of my experience enough to watch what I'm experiencing while I'm experiencing it. It's switching my attention to awareness itself rather than just having my attention on what I'm aware of. I watch my own thoughts or emotions rather than being caught up in them. I switch from thinking about life to experiencing it more directly.

There is no method for witnessing. It's like thinking I need to know how to open my eyes when they're closed. There is no how-to about it. I just open my eyes.

Witnessing allows me to feel what I'm feeling even when those emotions include terror, shame, rage, or despair. I learn how to feel intensity without acting out these intense feelings in my daily life.

Advantages of Being Real

Being Real involves my willingness to communicate openly and honestly to others about what I'm feeling. It's about feeling the vitality that comes with open communication, rather than the dullness that comes with telling others only what I'm thinking.

Being Real is about my willingness to settle conflicts before they crystallize into the hardening of my heart.

Being Real means I don't have to talk down to children. Or talk up to people I admire. Or talk around the truth. Or talk behind people's backs. It's about my refusal to participate in third party talk unless it's uplifting.

In Being Real, I get to experience how simple it is to speak from my heart, how good it feels to be authentic, and how smoothly words come to me when I am.

It includes sensing when others are not being authentic with me, feeling when their words lack sincerity. I learn how to follow timbre and tone more than the words themselves.

Being Real is about my maintaining strong boundaries around people and organizations that feed off the energies of others.

It means letting go of relationships that are not meant to be, where the round peg no longer fits into the square hole no matter how much I want it to.

Being Real means using fewer words and making my word good.

It includes being sincere in answering the questions that matter most: Am I doing work I love or settling for work because of the money it pays? Am I taking care of my body or pretending my body doesn't care? Am I enjoying life now or postponing my enjoyment for later?

Finding out why I procrastinate or fear taking action is integral to my Being Real. So is expanding beyond that which keeps me small. I become a student of my own addictive tendencies, so that my addictions bring me face to face with what I fear most.

Being Real includes telling myself the truth about death so that I reverse the cultural taboo of ignoring the reality of death in daily life.

I use the awareness of death to awaken to life.

Being Real is refusing to be in denial about the collective problems and promise of planetary change: being honest about the immensity of the global issues facing us, and responding to these issues in ways that are personally real to me. It's about my refusing to deny the extreme seriousness of climate change and economic disparity, or thinking that the war over there doesn't involve me over here. It's letting go of the belief that more information and better technology will solve all our problems, when it's really consciousness that needs to evolve.

Being Real is aligning with what *is,* rather than what I think should be. Then, paradoxically, it's working to change what I don't like if it is within my power to do so.

Facing all this directly and intentionally, and then feeling the emotions that come with it, is Being Real. This authenticity allows me to better offer my gifts to the world in response to what's happening within it.

More than anything else, Being Real is letting go of the misperception that I am a separate, body-defined being, and replacing it with the reality that I am connected to Everything.

Connected to Everything. Ah! The perfect bridge into the Fourth Way of Being.

DOWN TO THIS

After you've done everything you can
After you've searched unsuccessfully
As a bug
As a bird
As a good and bad person
For a way out of the maze
For your ticket to redemption
Doesn't it boil down to this?

You must be willing
To sit in Hell
As long as it takes
To find light
And delight
In the Fire.

7

BEING CONNECTED
Can I Give and
Receive Love?

Adam and Eve Were Sweeties

Adam and Eve were sweeties. They lived in a non-dual, timeless reality in which everything was connected within the infinite Oneness of life. Their home was a place called Eden. In Hebrew, Eden means *delightful*, and it perfectly describes the glorious garden reality in which they lived.

Being seamlessly connected to one another, Adam and Eve had no marital problems. Since they had no self-awareness, clothing was optional. And because they had whatever they wanted, they had no desires.

The only problem with living in the Garden of Eden was that they didn't know they were in it. There wasn't anything outside of it. There was no contrast between Eden and anywhere else. Adam and Eve lived in a perfect world without being aware of its perfection. They had no way of knowing how happy they were. They were not self-aware, and had no sense of their place within the Whole.

At some point in the evolution of things, the innate intelligence of Life knew that self-awareness was an essential experience for Adam and

Eve to have. For that to happen, they had to leave Eden—their Oneness state—and become differentiated. They had to become individualized. They had to seemingly separate from each other and from the Whole. I say "seemingly separate" because they didn't really leave the Garden, Oneness, or each other. It would have been impossible to leave what they were an intrinsic part of. Being separate was an illusion. But it was a strong, powerful illusion—one that can be just as confusing to any of us today as it was to Adam and Eve.

Adam and Eve differentiated through the development of their cerebral cortexes. They developed their capacity to think. This evolutionary leap was symbolically represented by the Tree of Knowledge. Eve was the one to catch onto the thinking thing first, which is where *the snake* comes in.

Because of its wondrous capacity to shed its own skin, the snake is an archetypal symbol of evolutionary change. People who have a problem with change refer to the snake as the serpent of the Devil. Eve was highly into change; she wasn't afraid when the snake offered her a bite of the apple freshly plucked from the Tree of Knowledge. Fully trusting Eve, Adam saw what she was eating and joined her in finishing off the apple.

Because creation stories almost never concern themselves with time, we don't know whether this next part happened immediately or over the next one hundred thousand years: Adam and Eve started to think more and more rationally and conceptually. This meant that while they were directly experiencing life, they could also think about it. They could represent what they were experiencing with words and thus share their experiences, ideas, solutions, desires, frustrations, hopes, and dreams with each other. They could put their thoughts together. They could imagine and create. They could communicate.

Before long, Adam and Eve had all kinds of thoughts about anything and everything. They gave things names and named themselves. The more they did so, the more things became differentiated.

As with anything new, there was a period of adjustment during which they were both completely caught up in this new rational thinking phenomenon. Being able to simultaneously feel their connection to the Whole was temporarily put on hold. This is like today with texting. We can text one another and forget to talk face to face. But texting is new. Forgetting to talk with one another while we text is temporary. Hopefully.

As time went on, Adam got caught up in thinking a bit more than Eve. The jobs he took on required some pretty intense thinking and problem solving. Since separation gives rise to competition and a new set of needs, he had to figure out how to keep the family safe and where to hunt for their food. The intensity of his thinking eventually led to over-thinking, which led to constant thinking. With this, he lost some of his ability to feel the life he was thinking about. This included a decreased ability to feel Eve. There is no blame here. It just happened that way.

At some point, Adam began to think it was Eve's fault that they were no longer in the Garden of Eden. After all, she took the first bite of the apple. Although Eve got caught in thought as well, she managed to better balance the old Oneness paradigm with the new Individuation paradigm. Her balance allowed her to multi-task: to keep an eye on the kids, cook the food, stay out of Adam's way when he was cranky—all of this while still accessing the Oneness of her garden-heart. She kept getting memory flashes not only *of* the Garden of Eden, but also that she *was* the Garden of Eden.

Here, the story veers off in two directions. In one direction, Eve completely forgets about the Garden. She falls under Adam's domination and ends up wearing a beauty-pageant bikini in Las Vegas or a full-body burka in Baghdad.

In the alternative direction, Eve continues to hold the vision of Oneness through every witch-hunt and rape, until dawn lights up the morning sky again.

Adam and Eve Story Reflections

Both Adam and Eve are always doing the best they can possibly do. This individuate-then-connect-up-again thing is a tough one.

Fast forward to today. The Garden of Eden is threatened. The water is no longer pure. Many of the forests within it have been cleared. Its food fields have been turned into battlefields. It's in deep disarray.

But recently something quite extraordinary has begun to happen. Inexplicably, both Adam and Eve have started to vividly remember some of the things they forgot back when they first began to differentiate. They are getting glimpses of the original code. Both are now saying—and even singing—to the other, "We've got to get ourselves back to the Garden."

It's uncertain exactly how the Adam and Eve story unfolds from here. Will they restore the Garden in time? Will they really become full-on sweeties and live happily ever after? None of this is clear.

What is clear is that in this creation story we are not the descendants of Adam and Eve. We *are* Adam and Eve. Together, we are continuing to decide how the story unfolds.

Smile if you know this.

Difficulties of Being Connected in a Disconnected Culture

What if, for thousands of years, 99.999 percent of us have been able to experience ourselves *only* as individuated beings? What if our perception for all these years would have us accept this statement as true: "I am here and the tree is over there"? What if we've believed that experiencing ourselves as separate from everything else is the only way to experience life? What if we've believed our perception of being separate from everything is actually the way life is because that's how it looks to us? In a perceptual nutshell, how could the tree possibly be me? To say that it is would seem ridiculous.

Two similar examples of this kind of perceptual confusion involve how we experience our planet. When I look around in any direction, the world definitely looks flat to me. I know it's not flat; science tells me so and I've seen pictures of it from space. Still, regardless of what I know conceptually, the world appears flat. Also, the world looks like it's not moving, when it is actually flying around the sun at a mind-blowing rate of 67,000 miles per hour. Examples like this remind me that my perception of things doesn't always match up with the reality of things.

As science has confirmed that the earth is round and moving quickly through space, it has also confirmed that what we perceive as solid objects—which clearly seem to be separate from one another—are not solid or separate at all. They and we are made of energy moving in different configurations and speeds, in one vast energetic field of light.

What if we can expand our sensory perception to directly experience ourselves as light, connected to this vast energetic field? At the same time, what if we can still maintain the ability to experience ourselves as solid, individuated beings?

Carrying the what-if a little further, suppose this expanded perceptual capacity to feel our connection to the whole of life automatically came with a cascade of immediate, life altering experiences. Imagine the possibilities:

- We would have an instantaneous, joyful sense of relief and gratitude that we no longer have to struggle against life, because we experience that we're an integral part of it. We'd begin to relax in ways we never before thought possible.

- We would receive an immediate flood of love for people and nature because we are literally, not figuratively, experiencing that we are everyone and everything. We'd move within a sense of endless wonder, as we see all of life is one continuous miracle, and that we are one with what created us.

- We would experience a dissolution of the fears, self-doubts, and traumatic memories that had their origins in our feeling like we were only a separated self, cut off from the rest of the life. Somehow, we'd now know that life doesn't end in death. We just change forms.

If these what-ifs come true, it will mean we have made it back to the Garden of Eden, but this time, we return as self-aware, individuated people who are able to consciously experience the unity and perfection of life.

Instead of focusing on the party we would throw to celebrate this beautiful perceptual leap, I want to briefly focus first on some of the social difficulties that come with returning to the Garden. Perhaps some of these difficulties are already familiar to you. If so, you will know why we are putting a temporary hold on the party.

No Words

As mentioned at the beginning of the book, there are millions of people awakening, right now, all around the planet. But we haven't yet come up with a name for these people who are in the process of awakening. Without a distinct name, there is no easy way to differentiate them from the people who are not yet awakening or from those who are already awake (saints, enlightened beings, etc.). As a result, it is next to impossible to talk with one another about this evolutionary leap in consciousness. Also, without language to identify this developmental phenomenon, *awakening-ones* can find it difficult to fully identify themselves as *awakening-ones*. They have no mental framework for it. I don't think Raven's napkin names of *conscious adult* and *conscious conduit* are going to become the names we end up with, but at least he's naming what has been unnamed.

We also don't have adequate words to describe the differences in perceptual experience that *awakening-ones* and *not-yet-awakening-ones* are experiencing. To begin with, most of our languages have been developed by *not-yet-awakening-ones*. (See how clumsy these terms are?) As such, they reflect the perception of their speakers. They are mostly organized around subject and object. For example, in English, it is difficult to say anything without automatically speaking from the perceptual viewpoint that everything is separated from everything else. If I say, "I see the mountain," it implies that there is a definite, distinct "me" who sees a definite, distinct "mountain." I have no easy way of saying "I am the mountain that I am seeing."

In "Connected-English," which hasn't been developed yet, we would have words that represent the union of subject with object. We'd have to start at the very beginning by coming up with a different word for "I"— and all the other pronouns—that would communicate the difference between people experiencing themselves as connected to everything from those experiencing themselves as separated from everything.

Communication between *awakening-ones* and ones *not-yet awakening* is extremely difficult without words to describe perceptual differences. Just as eagles can see things from the air that we can't, and dogs can hear sounds we can't, *awakening-ones* can perceive the connectivity of all things that others in the mass culture don't. Because they can't perceive in this way, the mass culture folks have no frame of reference for what the awakening folks are experiencing. If one says to the other, with great passion and joy, "Everything is One!", the person not yet awakening will think the other is either spaced out or on drugs. If you are a *Cool Hand Luke* movie fan, you'll remember the famous line the prison superintendent said to Luke right before he shot him—"What we have here is a failure to communicate." Bang!

We could stop right here and say, "Hmm ... we have a problem. How does someone seeing color talk to someone only seeing black and white?"

In regular English, we also have a major problem with words like "God." There's a tendency to use this word as a noun. As soon as God is reduced to a noun, "God" loses the original meaning of being beyond description. This has important consequences. By turning God into a person, place, thing, or idea, I'm automatically making God outside of or separate from me. The moment I do this, I'm tempted to decide if God is a He, a She, or an It. I also have to place God somewhere spatially.

If I come from a paternalistic culture, I'll envision God as a *He*. Then I'll have to decide where I think *He* resides. I'll need another word for that—*Heaven*, perhaps—and imagine that *He* lives in *Heaven*, which is above me. This means that now I'm down here on earth separated from Him up there in Heaven. Still in a dualistic world, God and Heaven must have their opposites, so I then need a *Devil*, which I also imagine to be masculine, and then a place where the Devil hangs out: *Hell*. The Devil lives in Hell, which I believe to be an *actual place* somewhere below me. It's an infinitely terrible place where people are imprisoned forever by God, Our Father… who art in Heaven.

Again, living in this mental, dualistic reality has serious implications. I can spend my entire life in fear that God will not approve of me and that my death will end in eternal damnation. Telling people this morbid story is cruel. It becomes a sadistic means of control by authority figures who pretend to know who is saved and who isn't.

In Gurmukhi, a "connected-language" created by Sikh mystics, the most-often used name for God is *Wahe Guru*, which means "Wow!" *Wow* is often the expression of someone having a God-moment, or the experience of coming out of separation into Oneness. As a name for God, it frees God from the ridiculously narrow confines of being a noun.

All of this conceptual separation of things can seem true to the people who aren't yet experiencing interconnection. It can also seem totally absurd to the *awakening-ones* who are having a completely different perceptual experience.

Creating connected-language will happen on its own as more of us awaken into connection. It's just a matter of time. Scientists had to find a new word for the kind of physics that described connected-reality. They chose the word "quantum" and placed it in front of "physics" to provide themselves, and us, with another way to talk about the unified field we are all part of. We had no need for the term "global warming" or "climate change" until enough people were feeling the heat. Now that we have an urgent need to talk about it, we're coming up with new words to do so.

Parallel Reality Clash

The *not-yet-awakening-ones* and the *awakening-ones* will often see each other as being from different planets. What they each do and believe often doesn't make sense to the other. I'll mention three examples to represent the endless list of differences.

Not-yet-awakening-ones will primarily tend to see life *conceptually* through the lens of thought: through the mind. They think about life more than they feel it. They may consider their thoughts and beliefs important enough to sacrifice themselves or their loved ones, proclaiming that they will defend the honor of their country and their faith to their very last breath. In conceptual reality, beliefs are serious things.

The *awakening-ones* tend to live more in experiential reality than in conceptual reality. They feel life more than they think about it. Beliefs, in general, are often just thoughts. Therefore, to them, beliefs can seem archaic. There is no longer a need to believe in something that simply *is;* i.e., there's no need to believe in elephants, or in the future, or in sunrises.

Another example of perceptual difference between our two groups is that many *not-yet-awakening-ones* will believe that those who have billion-dollar bank accounts are smart and successful. Most *awakening-ones* will perceive the super-rich as over-consumers who haven't explored their need for so much money and power. They would point out that Jesus probably wouldn't own three homes and a yacht, that he said something about selling your yacht and giving the proceeds to the poor. The *not-yet-awakening-ones* would say that Jesus never said anything about yachts, so what's the problem?

In the past, political parties primarily represented people with differences in opinion. Now, there are signs that political parties are increasingly representing people operating from different levels of awareness. The *not-yet-awakening-ones* are congregating in more conservative parties that articulate policies favoring law and order, national security, corporate power, military strength, traditional family and religious values, and restricted immigration. The focus is on a political agenda that presumes our separation. The *awakening-ones* are drawn to liberal parties that articulate policies favorable to community policing, social justice, equitable income distribution, international cooperation, military restraint, climate change policy, non-traditional family and spiritual values, and more porous national borders. The focus here is on politics that recognize our connection.

This is new. It's a cultural, spiritual, political polarization that will increase as the evolutionary process of awakening continues.

Hitler Confusion

The differences between the *not-yet-awakening-ones* and the *awakening-ones* go well beyond one belief system colliding with another, as we see in contrasting religions or political parties of the past. I'm referring to one group of people evolving into a more highly developed perceptual awareness, ahead of those who aren't. Yet. This "yet" is important. Everyone is evolving; there are just differences in the time-frame in which this evolution is occurring.

To frame Heart Awakening as a more highly evolved level of perceptual awareness will almost certainly be met with anger and fear by many people, religious or not. They may hear it as similar to what Hitler said about Germans being superior to other people, or what some Hindus still believe about one caste being superior to another caste.

The evolutionary change I'm referring to has nothing to do with some people being superior or better than others. It has to do with a massive change in perception. *Awakening-ones* are not better than *not-yet-awakening-ones.* They just perceive the unity of life more easily than those who don't. Dogs are not better than we are because they hear sounds we can't. They simply hear sounds we can't.

Crucifying Non-Believers

Ironically, the religious and fundamentalist *not-yet-awakening-ones* can sometimes feel the most threatened by the *awakening-ones.* For example, as I'm using the terms, Jesus was a fully *awakened-one* and the priests who opposed him were *not-yet-awakening-ones.* His story shows the depth of the threat the *awakening-ones* and *awakened-ones* pose to the belief systems of the *not-yets.* He was tortured and killed. "What we have here is a failure to communicate." Bang!

But our mass Culture of Separation is dramatically changing. If I own a business selling fast food that makes people unhealthy, my business must crumble as people start listening to their own bodies, rather than to my dishonest happy-ads. Closer to home, if I have made it my life's work to criticize myself every time I get a chance, my life will change as I relax and love those parts of me that I previously deemed unworthy of love.

Without having access to the reality of connection, some people will need more and more power and stuff as the old systems crash. Others will need the mental certainty of fanaticism, or the chemical bliss of cocaine, or the paralyzing trance of chronic poverty. Any of these things are needed just to get through the night, when survival of the fittest is the only game in town. Living in separation and duality *is* hell.

Being Connected

Instead of being the sun, I strike a match and call it me.

Feeling separate from life always generates fear. It's the nature of the beast. But when we come into connection, the fear softens, as does our need to control things. Fear and control are replaced with an innate desire to cooperate and co-create.

So, what do we *do* to personally end this Myth of Separation? The possible responses to this question are infinite. My personal responses may seem frustrating to some, as they all involve some sort of inquiry or introspection rather than doing something. They all involve the willingness to feel what's normally avoided—feeling how it feels to be disconnected. I have several ways for how I access feeling my own disconnection.

The first way involves my willingness to drop down into my body and notice what I feel. When I do this, I may discover mental chatter, low-grade anxiety, high-grade unworthiness, general numbness, an inability to sense my environment, a tight solar plexus, and even all of these at once. I've learned that these feelings *are* disconnection. This is what disconnection feels like! I've also learned that these feelings are so normalized within me that I often have difficulty recognizing them as disconnection. I'll just think they are the reality of life. The trick is to witness what I normally feel most of the time and then question its veracity. Disconnection hides in the normalcy of the everyday experience of it.

There is one other catch to feeling our disconnected state. As soon as we start feeling it, it can quickly turn into something that feels terrible—so terrible that we won't want to continue feeling it. Instead, we'll want to go make a peanut butter and jelly sandwich and check our texts. Or we'll want to listen to the thoughts that start shouting that there is no such thing as disconnection, so why are we just sitting here doing nothing?

It won't work if we listen to our own reasons to *avoid* feeling our disconnection. Nor will affirmations be useful in this realm; positive thinking can keep us away from experiencing disconnection just as much as negative thinking does. Chanting mantras will often hypnotize us rather than take us deeper into feeling it. Concentrating on breathing can often help us get in touch with disconnection, but the temptation will then be to focus on breathing *instead* of feeling the terrible discomfort of that disconnection.

Personally, I just have to sit and feel this disconnection, until a very strange thing happens. The sense of it can move from feeling *terrible*, to feeling a bit *interesting*. This *interesting* feeling often pops up in full view, then slinks back until it comes up again later. At some point, however, my feeling disconnected shifts from being terrible, into being interesting, even fascinating. When it reaches the point of being fascinating, it can come with an incredible discovery: "Oh, *this* is what I've been feeling all my life! I've been feeling my own disconnection! Isn't that the most amazing thing? I can actually feel my own disconnection!"

As this happens, my disconnection turns into connection. I connect with the disconnection. When I'm fully willing to face the dragon I most fear, the dragon turns into a powerful Uber-dragon-pet-friend that will fly me anywhere I want to go, free of charge. But making this switch into fascination is so much easier said than done. Actually, it's not very easily said, either. I had to struggle with how to describe feeling my own disconnection. Again, we don't have language for all of this yet.

How else do I come into feeling connected? My second answer is related to feeling my disconnected state. If I'm with a good friend, I can ask myself if I'm actually *feeling* love for this person, right now, in the moment. I'm not asking whether I love him or her, because my mind will probably say, "Of course I do!" and that will be the end of that inquiry. The question is whether or not I'm actually feeling love for this person right now.

Feeling in-this-moment love comes with a very distinct, unmistakable sensation that most of us are familiar with. I can *know* or *think* I love someone, yet not necessarily feel the unmistakable sensation that comes with this love-thought. If I don't feel in-the-moment love, I may feel neutral or even numb toward that person—not love, but not not-love: neutral.

If I'm willing to let myself feel this absence of love as it is, without a judgment that I should be feeling love or that I am a faulty person because I can't feel love, I can explore what this love-numbness feels like. This takes tremendous courage. I have to be totally honest with myself and admit that I don't feel love. Admitting that I don't love as much as I *think* I do can call up my inner critic: my S.W.A.T. team that has a shoot-first-ask-later policy within my own psyche. "I'm supposed to be a loving person, so why don't I feel love right now? There is obviously something wrong with me." This can be even more difficult for people who take on roles in which people expect them to be loving: clergy, spouses, parents, care-givers, spiritual teachers. It's even harder for these people to question their own love-feeling state because they are supposed to be loving. For parents to face that they are not actually *feeling love* for their children can be terrifying. They may then *think* they don't love their children, rather than realize they are not feeling the love they actually do have for their children.

If I stay with this inquiry and surrender to the reality of my own love limitations, something unforeseen can happen. I can realize that what I've been labeling as non-love is actually *frozen* love. It can dawn on me that there is only love, and that I am either feeling that love or feeling love in its disconnected, frozen form. But frozen love is still love, just as ice is still water. This realization alone can thaw out what I've have held frozen within me from an early age.

I want to mention one more important thing about re-connecting to connection. To connect to everything, I must be willing to receive love. I must become suspicious of how comfortable I am giving to others, and how uncomfortable I am in receiving. I have to be honest about the possibility that I *give* love to stay away from *receiving* it. I've known myself to be that clever.

How many times do I have to feel disconnection before I feel connection? In my experience, I must do it as often as it keeps coming up. At this point in my life, I've stopped counting. However, I've learned that feeling my own disconnection is my most reliable portal into connection. And connection is love.

Being Clear, Present, Real, and Connected leads to the Fifth Way of Being. It's the grand finale.

WHICH IS WHICH

Have you ever seen a fly on a horse?
I'm talking about an itsy, bitsy little fly
Perched on the back
Of a big, strong horse
Where one's so small
And the other's so large.

Just like your mind
And your heart—
One tiny
The other vast.

But in you
Which one is which?
Is your heart the one's that's little
While your mind is bloated with thought?
Or is your mind dwarfed
By your ever-expanding heart?

Get this ratio right
And you can fly free
And horse around forever.

8

BEING HEART-DIRECTED
What Do I Truly Want?

The Colonel's House

I began my Circle facilitation work by forming men's groups in the Eighties and Nineties. I called them Men in Circle. Men in Circle provided men with a safe place to share things about themselves that they might not ordinarily share. It also gave them a chance to find out what they truly wanted in life rather than what they were conditioned to want.

One night in Circle, in a very dramatic and hushed voice, a retired Air Force Colonel and former fighter jet pilot said he wanted to share something he had never shared with anyone before. It was about what he had wanted his entire life. No one in the Circle knew why he had been so chronically secretive about this. It was obviously a big stretch for him to reveal it. He proceeded to tell us that he wanted to build his own dream house on a small lake in Michigan, two hundred miles north of Detroit. He shared in great detail what it would look like and where it would be on the lake. He spoke reverentially and had tears in his eyes as he painted this dream-house picture in his hushed-tone voice.

As he continued to speak, I began to notice that, despite his tears and hushed words, I couldn't feel any real emotion in what he was saying. I wasn't moved by his vision. It felt flat to me. As my certainty about this increased, so did my dread. Could I possibly tell him that his words weren't moving me? I didn't know if I had the courage to be real with him about this, given that we were the first people he had ever shared it with, and given the tears and tenderness coming from him as he spoke.

Being Real is a big part of what we do in Circle together. Since we had agreed that we all wanted to be authentic, I decided to risk it. When he finished, I quietly told him, "I can't feel any juice in what you just shared."

My statement was followed by an eerie silence. No one spoke for at least a minute, which is a long time to wait for something to explode. Then, suddenly, he reacted the way I thought he might. He got enraged! I can still remember the angry, hurt, bullet words he fired at me as only a fighter pilot could.

During a pause in his barrage, I managed to raise my head up long enough to ask him if he was willing to trust me for a couple of minutes. Reluctantly he said, "Yes, but only for three minutes." Three minutes. He was a pretty precise man. Must have come with the training. Anyway, I asked the rest of the men in the Circle if they were willing to trust me as well. I knew they thought I'd made a huge mistake by saying what I said to the Colonel, and they didn't know how this was going to end. I didn't either.

I asked him if he was willing to get still for a moment, along with rest of us, to look into the possibility that there may be an even deeper desire underneath his desire to build his home. He said he'd try this. Reluctantly. For three minutes. The rest of the men agreed, and a few of us smiled as we saw him set the timer on his watch. Although I had no idea whether he'd actually connect with a deeper longing, I have learned to trust my gut intuition in tense situations like these.

Within thirty seconds of shutting his eyes, he suddenly burst out laughing. We all started laughing with him, having no idea why. After he caught his breath, he told us he had an immediate realization. He realized that he wasn't building this house for himself. He was building it to win approval from his ultra-critical father, who just happened to be a retired homebuilder. He saw that what he really wanted was to build something better than his father had built.

And then he started to sob. Through his tears, he shared that, underneath everything, the only thing he ever wanted was for his dad to say to him, "You did well, son. I'm proud of you."

We all felt the authenticity in what he was sharing. Several of the Circle members ended up crying with him. Most of us knew this father-want well.

The Colonel's House Story Reflections

The Fifth Way of Being is Being Heart-Directed. The way I'm using the term, Heart-Directed is not about loving others. It's about inquiring into what we truly want from moment to moment and then making choices around those want, instead of making choices around what we have been conditioned to want. Heart Awakening requires this. It isn't optional.

In the English language, the words "want" and "desire" are extremely loaded when used in a religious or spiritual context. For example, in *The Power of Now*, Eckhart Tolle says that to find happiness in life we have to stop wanting; we have to get rid of all desires.

On the other hand, the Abraham-Hicks teachings say that happiness in life actually begins when we start aligning with our desires. Being in touch with what we want is what brings us to life. It is the fulfillment of our creative nature, akin to Joseph Campbell's encouragement to *follow your bliss*. Over centuries of spiritual tradition, this paradox has led to a great deal of confusion and suffering.

From my own experience, Tolle and Abraham-Hicks are saying the same thing, but their frames of reference for "want" and "desire" are different. Tolle is talking about getting rid of conditioned wants, that following them only leads to suffering. Abraham-Hicks is talking about following what we truly want—desires that come from the heart rather than the conditioned mind.

We all make thousands of decisions daily around what we want. What do we want to do, think, feel, have, be? We are creative beings, given free choice around all categories of wanting, every minute of the day. The choices we make create the quality of our life. Am I making choices from my conditioning or from my heart?

Difficulties of Being Heart-Directed in a Mind-Directed Culture

Strangely enough, even though knowing what we truly want is crucial to living a joyful, productive life, there is almost no meaningful dialogue or intentional training around how we go about choosing what we want. We are not given a personal foundation from which to meaningfully choose from moment to moment.

In school, there is no class that teaches how we distinguish between our conditioned wants and our heart-felt wants. Nor is there guidance for knowing what to do when the urge to follow our conditioned desires is far stronger than our real desires. For example, children are totally on their own when it comes to sorting out the kind of false advertising images that show only healthy-looking people eating junk food.

The difficulty continues from here. We have created such a vast array of material choices in life that it appears as if we have all the freedom we could ever want. Yet in reality, it turns out, these are false freedoms. Do we want regular fries or super-sized? Do we want a cell phone with 4.7-inch or 5.5-inch Retina HD display? Do we want to vacation in Miami, Maui, or Mexico?

This gets even more complex. No matter what we think we want, and no matter who we are or how old we are, what we all want is some version of the same thing: we want to feel good. We make most of our decisions based on whether we believe what we choose will make us feel better or feel worse.

As I mentioned earlier, two of the primary difficulties we face are the speed of change and the vast over-stimulation which come with electronic life. There is an ever-increasing, unprecedented pressure on our nervous systems that we can't put a finger on because it's so pervasive. Instead of floating down a river as in times past, we're trying to run up a water slide. We are vaguely aware of this change, even though the culture isn't verifying our experience of it.

Being chronically over-stressed feels really, really bad. When we're stressed, we tend to choose what we want based on what will give us the quickest relief from stress. There's a host of familiar things we can choose to make us feel instantly better: sugar, caffeine, sex, video games, the news, eating, consuming, thinking, alcohol, drugs, over-working, emotional venting, texting, extreme sports, gambling, or reading. Even cutting oneself can relieve stress in a strange sort of way. The list goes on and on.

When the collective stress level is as astronomically high as it is today, our first desire will often be to find a way out of the tension. When we ask ourselves what we want, we may think we want a large glass of wine after work, but what we really want is to relax; to feel good. Alcohol or highly caffeinated energy drinks can provide this instantly, but the obvious problem is that these kinds of stress relievers end up wreaking additional havoc on our nervous systems which are already dangerously overloaded. Our instant fix turns into a super-stressor that makes it even more difficult to relax. We grow dependent on the fix which further stresses our system, and the cycle gets more vicious. Once in this cycle, "where she stops, nobody knows."

We aren't yet openly talking about any of this with each other. We end up waging war on drugs without an overview-understanding of its underlying cause.

What we can do is return to the most basic of human inquiries: In this moment, what do I truly want? What do I base my choice on? Is what I think I want truly what I want, or just a trick of my mind or my desperate need to relax?

We come into ever-deepening transformation when this inquiry becomes conscious, intentional, and ever-present: when Being Heart-Directed becomes a way of being in life.

Being Heart-Directed

There is a linear order to the Five Ways of Being. And there is a reason why Being Heart-Directed is the last of these elemental inquiries. In order to inquire into what I truly want, it's essential that I have a sound framework for my inquiry. The other Four Ways of Being can provide such a framework. To Be Heart-Directed requires the synergistic inquiries of the other four ways.

- Being Clear: Knowing what my purpose is has a direct impact on what I want. If my life purpose is simply to survive, I'll want whatever it takes to get through the night. If my purpose is to open to love, I'll want whatever furthers that. On a more mundane level, if my purpose in eating is to be healthy, I'll obviously want to eat healthy foods. If I eat to relieve stress, I'll want that soda with its sixty-six grams of sugar. My conscious or subconscious purpose directly impacts what I want and don't want.

  Knowing my purpose can eventually become the foundation for choosing what I want. I simply keep the question in the forefront of my awareness. Does what I want right now serve my purpose, or not? This doesn't mean I'm going to automatically choose what serves my purpose, but at least I have a framework for choosing that goes beyond my conditioned or addictive wants.

- **Being Present:** I can't know what I truly want unless I can move out of my chattering mind and the conditioned thoughts that come with it. What I truly want often emerges from stillness. It comes in the form of intuitive flashes, or as a simple, inner knowing. The wants that come from stillness will feel alive and clear. Wants that come from my chattering mind will feel dry, itchy, or sticky. I must develop my relationship with stillness in order to know the difference between the two.

- **Being Real:** In order to know what I truly want, I need to feel what I'm feeling. If I'm depressed and don't know it, I'll want to stay away from people without knowing why. If I'm angry and don't know it, I'll want to take my anger out on others, often without being aware that I am. If I'm truly happy, I'll want to follow what sustains my happiness.

- **Being Connected:** In order to know what I want, I need to access the experiential realities of life: that I am loved, that life is not a perpetual struggle, that people are inherently good, that I am a sovereign being living within an Infinite Self.

All this leads to Being Heart-Directed. Being Heart-Directed doesn't mean all my desires go away. That happens when I die, maybe. It means I am free to prefer one thing to another, because that preference or desire is aligned with my purpose. At some point, what I truly want comes full circle. What I ultimately want is to awaken, which, to me, means being Clear, Present, Real, Connected, and Heart-Directed.

To inquire into what I truly want often needs plenty of space for failure, wrong answers, or for no answers at all. Inquiry requires tenacity and courage. It also requires a sense a humor, because paradox is at play here. Finding out what I truly want is the easiest, most natural thing in the world. It can also be the most difficult thing in the world.

I want to mention two more important notes about Being

Heart-Directed. In looking at what I want, it's essential that I add these words to my inquiry: "*Given what's given, …*" what do I truly want? I facilitated a man in Circle who had polio as a child and didn't have use of his badly atrophied legs. He was a very discouraged middle-aged man. When I asked him what he wanted, he said that he just wanted his legs to work so he could walk. Given the givens, this was not likely to happen. The question remained, "Given that you are not likely to walk, what do you want?" Without considering what's given, we can go into magical thinking. This is a set-up for disappointment and despair.

Closely related is this second point: If I fervently want someone else to change, or external circumstances to change, my wanting won't lead to anything positive. If I want my partner to be more this or that, or that there be warm weather for my next camping trip, I am knocking on a door that isn't designed to open.

The Advantages of Being Heart-Directed

Being Heart-Directed is not just confined to my own wants. It includes my wanting others to have what they truly want. My heart is designed to entrain with other hearts, like birds in flight changing directions in silence together. The birds are not codependent, abdicating their own wants for the wants of the other birds in flight. They fly in formation from their connectedness, as we all do when we experience our heart connection to others. Being Heart-Directed opens up the possibility of entraining with others without relinquishing personal sovereignty. Strong communities are made of this.

Within the Culture of Separation, we have a hand-me-down notion that our happiness is dependent upon our wants being met. "I'll be happy when…" and "I'll be happy if…" are alternating refrains to the song that never ends well for those who sing it.

When we are heart-directed, our happiness increases as we follow what we want. At the same time, our happiness no longer depends on getting what we want. Who could want more than this?

Summary

We're now going to take a giant leap from the Five Ways of Being to look at how we can change the social groups we're in so that they support us in being Clear, Present, Real, Connected, and Heart-Directed with one another. But before we go there, I want to briefly summarize these last eight chapters. The summary itself will help provide an introduction to how we can intentionally create "awakening-friendly" relationships and social groups:

- Heart Awakening is an evolutionary leap of perception in which we experience the unity of life while still maintaining our individual sovereignty. It gives us access to greater love, joy, and creative wisdom.

- We are at a crossroads in history. Centuries of collective heart-numbing and disconnection, combined with extreme technological change, have created a planetary crisis that threatens our survival.

- Our way through this crisis is in the continuation of our evolutionary leap into Love. Taking this leap gives us expanded capacities for peaceful, co-creative problem solving and sharing.

- In the past, only a handful of people awakened in any given time. Today millions of people are awakening at once.

- We are part of this awakening. It is happening through us. To us. Right now.

- My own exploration of Heart Awakening has led me to see how awakening can be defined so that the definition itself provides a living framework for awakening. The framework, and Heart Awakening itself, involves these Five Ways of Being:

Being Clear: What's my purpose?

Being Present: How do I quiet my mind and be still?

Being Real: What am I feeling right now?

Being Connected: Am I willing to give and receive love?

Being Heart-Directed: What do I truly want?

Ready to jump into the second half of this book?

Part II

WITH EVERYONE
AROUND US

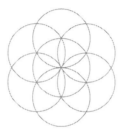

There are literally thousands upon thousands of teachers and teachings from all parts of the world that give us ways to awaken individually. All of these teachers and teachings organize around how we, as individuals, can become healthy, happy, and holy. Even if people live and practice together, the focus is still usually on the individual. Most members of ashrams, churches, weekend workshops, and group pilgrimages to holy sites are still focused on the question "How can I awaken?" rather than "How can we support one another so that we awaken together?" The focus has been on *my* body, *my* emotions, *my* health, *my* diet, and *my* consciousness. There is nothing wrong with this *me-centered* paradigm. It is as it should be. However, there is an entirely new spiritual paradigm beginning to supplement the me-centered one. The new paradigm organizes around *we* as well as *me.* Its organizational structure is the circle.

In the spiritual circle, emphasis is on creating a group field in which the intelligence, longing, empathy, dedication, commitment, and wisdom of each individual is unified with every other individual. The circle field itself can then become the teacher.

Instead of one special teacher or one specific set of teachings being solely responsible for uplifting the frequency of the individual, the circle can become an environment strong enough to uplift everyone within it. This replaces reliance on one person or teaching. It also can inspire individual and collective sovereignty. It opens up the possibility for exponential personal and collective change.

In the very center of the paradigm shift from "me" to "me and we" is the opportunity for transforming our primary relationships, families, schools, businesses, organizations, and even our nations, so that these existing groups provide the spiritual support we once solely found in the ashram, congregation, or inspirational workshop. Instead of having to leave our existing groups to find support for our awakening, we can learn how to create the spiritual support we need within them. Who needs to live in an ashram when we have friends that know how to create a circle field as powerful as an ashram? What can a guru add when a community works together to create a school devoted to the heart-awakening of every student, teacher and administrator within it? What happens when a nation can transform so that its core function, and the mutual agreement within it, is to support every citizen's desire for life, liberty and the pursuit of happiness?

There are two major obstacles in transforming our social groups and relationships so that they support Heart-Awakening. First, transforming groups is breathtakingly difficult. Second, we've never received any guidance as to how we go about doing this. Even though we are intrinsically woven into an endless number of groups in life, our culture teaches almost nothing about how groups work. We get no training in understanding what makes some groups a joy to be in and others a living hell. Why are some families functional and others a mess? What makes a marriage work? A non-profit organization? A neighborhood? A nation? For the most part, group functionality in our culture is hit or miss. Sometimes our groups work and sometimes they don't. Too often, they don't.

In our present-day Culture of Separation, we generally pay attention to how a group *functions* relative to how it fulfills its purpose. We measure the success of a school by the number of students who graduate. We measure a business's functionality according to the profit it generates. But very little intentional focus is given to how people relate to one another within these groups, or how we can create a healthy social environment for the sake of its members' happiness. Some progressive businesses spend sizable amounts of money on bringing people into functional teams, but usually only so that these teams can better maximize profit.

I've spent the last several decades exploring the question of what makes groups and relationships functional, healthy, and transformational. I probably know as much about transformational group dynamics as anyone on the planet. But what I know now will be miniscule compared to what most people will know about group dynamics in the next hundred years. We are just beginning to explore the possibilities that come with increased group awareness. I'm like Henry Ford who knew a lot about making cars in 1916. But what would he say if he were to visit a highly-automated Ford plant in Dearborn, Michigan today? He'd be humbled.

My purpose in writing the second half of this book is to share what I've discovered about making our social groups and relationships awakening-friendly. This requires seeing groups and relationships in a totally new way.

BLIND SERVICE

Don't think you're here to serve others
Doing good deeds
For people in separate bodies
Outside of your own.

Take a closer look
At the blind crone lady
You're so gallantly helping
Across the street right now.

Don't you see?
It's she who's helping you
Cross that street
As you hold onto her arm
With such care.
She's walking you
Through the dangerous traffic
Away from your misperception
That you are separated
From those you serve.

She knows on which side reality resides
And she knows who's serving whom.
Why else would she have tossed you
Her white walking cane
As she skipped back through the traffic
With such joy?

Be still and watch
As she patiently waits
For another Good Samaritan
Another soulful person
Who is just as kind
Just as determined
And just as ready as you are
To cross over
Into the Oneness
You have always longed for.

9

LOOKING AT GROUPS IN A NEW WAY

Bottle of Vodka

Last year I was in the United Kingdom, sitting in as a guest observer of a drug and alcohol rehabilitation session with twelve live-in clients and their two therapists. They were discussing what everyone was feeling about an incident that occurred the night before. Another client—now ex-client—had managed to sneak a bottle of vodka into his room and drink it.

Several of the clients were expressing how scared and angry they were that this person had threatened their sobriety, and thus their lives, by bringing alcohol into what they felt was the only safe space in their world. I was deeply moved by how raw and exposed they felt about this Vodka-man's violation.

One of the therapists asked whether they would report any future violation if they had knowledge of it, or if this would be "snitching." Several clients spoke up, vehemently claiming that it wouldn't be snitching; it would be protecting their space and their sobriety. Others disagreed; they felt that turning another person into the authorities was a greater violation.

I suggested that they had an opportunity, in that particular moment, for everyone to come into agreement, or not, about reporting this kind of violation in the remaining twenty-five days of their program. After an hour of passionate and heated discussion, everyone ended up agreeing they would report any alcohol or drug violation to the clinic managers.

By making this agreement together, they were no longer twelve, separate individuals fighting separately for their sobriety. They had become a functional group the moment they came into agreement about what they wanted as a group. They were pledging to keep their living space "clean" for themselves and each other. They were also connecting more deeply by listening to what each person wanted, and then by making a group decision through consensus.

Even more importantly, they realized they could use their group sessions to talk about other things they wanted for making their rehabilitation a success. They began to sense that they could intentionally create a safe space to discuss and support each other's recovery needs.

What they did not know at the time was that their small rehab group was beginning to fulfill the primary function of all groups—to provide mutual support for what each person truly wants by being in the group.

The Power of Group Agreements

Human interaction is largely governed by agreements we have with one another. There are millions of these agreements. Some of them we are conscious of; the vast majority of them we are not. For example, one of the most basic social agreements we make is to not harm one another when we interact. If we sit down for a family meal or go to a movie, we assume we are safe in each other's company because we have a do-no-harm agreement in place. We don't even think about this until someone disagrees and shows up at the dinner table or in a movie theater with an assault rifle and starts shooting.

Agreements inform every aspect of social life. We agree to stop at red lights, to wait our turn in line, to smell relatively good, to pay back a loan, to be sexual only under certain circumstances, to refer to each other by our given names. Another example of social agreement is: a youthful-looking genius in the U.S. comes up with a social networking program he calls *Facebook*, and within ten years, two billion people on the planet have agreed to use it to communicate with one another.

Cultures vary to some extent because they have a different set of agreements in play. Gang culture agreements differ from gay culture agreements. French culture agreements differ from those of Honduran culture. We have all kinds of agreements around the elderly, toddlers, the sick, the rich, and the poor. All of these vary according to the subcultures we're in.

Most of our agreements have been handed down from generation to generation. We learn about them through experiential osmosis more than through verbal instruction. They are essential to all social inter-action and foundational to what culture is. Some of these agreements have been frozen and compressed over time into taboos, laws, morals, beliefs, rules, expectations, demands, and codes of conduct. They make us think we have no choice but to agree with them, even though we always have choice. The question is whether or not we want to face the consequences of exercising our choice to disagree. For example, in many U.S. southern states, there was once an agreement between white people and black people that black people couldn't drink from the same fountain as white people. In the South, this agreement was in place since the beginning of drinking fountains. Both races agreed, even though one race was dominating the other through intimidation and state sponsored terror.

Then some black people got past the intimidation and their own fear and decided they weren't going to agree to use separate fountains, even if it meant being arrested, beaten, or killed. After many black people were arrested, beaten, and killed, Americans generally agreed that having separate water fountains according to race is as silly as having separate fountains for right-handed and left-handed people.

In several Middle Eastern countries, there is an agreement in place that men can dress however they want and that women can be killed if they don't dress like the men want them to dress.

Why is any of this important? Because if we want to change the culture, it actually means changing the cultural agreements we have with one another. Culture change is an agreement to change our agreements.

Our personal interface with social change happens through what you and I agree or disagree with, individually and collectively. If I want something to change in my culture, I directly participate in changing it by refusing to agree or comply with whatever that is and then agreeing and complying with something else. If people in the Culture of Separation have agreed to turn sporting events into a multi-billion-dollar business, I can disagree by not showing up at The Quicken Loans Arena with my $180 ticket for the big game. If you don't agree with slaughtering a billion cows each year, you are free to act and eat accordingly by expanding your vegetable garden and giving up meat.

When we are serious about wanting to create cultural change, we have to know what it is in the culture we are seeking to change. For example, if we have a flat tire, we don't say we have to change the car. We have to identify what specifically about the car needs changing: the tire. Likewise, if we want cultural change, we have to know what it is about the culture that needs changing: the agreements. Positive, cultural change is about changing flat, dysfunctional agreements we've made with one another. We change these agreements through non-compliance, withdrawal, or cooperative negotiation within the specific groups to which we belong.

Culture of Separation: Agreements Around Awakening

If we want to change our social groups within the Culture of Separation so they support Heart Awakening, we need to look at the conscious and unconscious agreements around awakening within those groups. Then we need to decide whether the existing agreements serve us. If they don't serve our awakening, we find new agreements that do.

Through the lens of the Five Ways of Being, Heart Awakening requires that we be clear about purpose, present in stillness, real about what we're feeling, connected in love, and heart-directed in following what we truly want. In looking at how the mass culture organizes itself around awakening, it's pretty easy to see that it actually has agreements in play that not only differ from what's needed to awaken, but are in direct opposition to what's needed. The agreements we have with one another in the vast majority of our families, schools, friendships, businesses, etc. essentially *keep us from* awakening. These are not usually conscious agreements, and when we do identify them, an amazing narcoleptic story is on display for anyone to read.

I'm aware that I'm speaking in broad generalities and that our culture is in the process of changing. Still, culturally we agree to:

- Avoid all inquiry into purpose
- Be busy by staying in continuous forward motion
- Be inauthentic by masking our feelings with each other
- Be disconnected by discouraging love's expression
- Be mind-directed by following our social conditioning together

Agreement to Avoid Inquiry into Purpose

Most groups in our current culture create little time for group members to talk about either the group's purpose or each member's purpose for being in the group. The absence of this kind of inquiry has been so normalized that most of us may question why we would even want to talk about these things. What good would it serve? For example, in school, none of my teachers ever talked about why we were in school or what we were being educated *for*. We were never asked what we wanted by being in school, and there was never a viable alternative to school.

In most businesses, employees and employers rarely sit together to talk about what each person's purpose is for being in it. The topic doesn't come up, as if the question has no relevance. Even in marriage, most couples spend little, if any, time inquiring into the purpose for their being together. There's an underlying agreement to stay away from this kind of interpersonal reflection.

There is no complaint here. I am simply saying that most families, schools and organizations don't yet support us in the essential task of *exploring* our personal or group purpose. Our culture discourages it by not giving it value, time, and attention.

Agreement to Avoid Stillness

In most of our social groups we agree to stay busy. Being sped-up and over-stimulated is normalized, so we don't have to feel how abnormal it is to move through life as quickly as we do. For example, we praise and reward *tireless* workers. Most organizational meetings are conducted without a trace of silence. Type A personalities run almost everything. The smart phone has become a physical extension of our over-active minds. In most of our social groups, silence has little say.

It's as though the mass culture is waiting for someone to yell out loudly enough for everyone to hear, "Can we all just stop? Even for a moment? Can we stop moving? Stop talking? Stop everything and just look around in silence?"

In a way, this happened in New York City when the Twin Towers came down. Metaphorically, everyone in the world stopped on 9/11 for one horrific moment. But instead of staying still to fully feel what happened and to understand why it happened, we in the U.S. rushed off to war. And we drew up plans to build something taller than the towers that fell. The people of terror started to plan their next suicide mission from hell. It wasn't yet time for us to collectively stop long enough to find wisdom.

Agreement to Hide Emotions

Instead of agreeing to Be Real, there is a subconscious, collective, cultural agreement in place to hide most of what we're feeling from ourselves and from each other. We agree to pretend that pretending is normal. It's difficult to keep a corporate job, maintain friendships, belong to a mainstream temple or church, and still know and speak the truth about what we're actually feeling and experiencing. We simply haven't agreed with our co-members that we want to be real with one another and thereby begin to make it socially safe to be so.

Agreement to Avoid Connection

In most of our social groups we discourage one another from opening to love and from feeling the inherent connection between everyone and everything. We subconsciously agree that any talk or mere mention of love, connection, or Oneness is strictly forbidden. We agree to view life as it appears physically—everything separate from everything else. We subconsciously agree to shame, shun, or marginalize anyone questioning this perceptual reality.

There is a classic cartoon depicting two fish in the ocean. One fish says to the other, "What's all this talk about water?" Applied to us, we might say, "What's all this talk about Oneness?" In the Culture of Separation, there is great reluctance to find out.

Agreement to Be Mind-Directed

Instead of agreeing to follow what we truly want and love, we agree in most of our social groups to follow what we've been conditioned to want. Most groups support their members in going along with what the group wants from them. Churches want congregants to adhere to their beliefs. Countries want their citizens to pledge allegiance to their flag. Many friends want their fellow friends to stay within the safe boundaries of certain behavior and thought.

Joseph Campbell's exhortation to follow our bliss encourages us to find and pursue what we truly want from moment to moment. The Culture of Separation turns "Follow your bliss!" into advertising campaigns selling Coca Cola and Cialis.

We unconsciously go along with these agreements with our family members, friends, school mates, business associates, church members, just to name a few of our social connections. As I mentioned many times in the previous chapters, most of these agreements have been in place for centuries. If we violate or try to change them, there is usually a price to pay.

For example, when I went to Canada instead of Vietnam, there was obviously no opportunity for me to have any meaningful dialogue with my local draft board. There's a bit of irony in this because draft boards were designed to be local so that draft board members would know the families of the draftees they were sending to war. My family was close to the head of the draft board's family. Yet there was never a chance for me to talk with him or the draft board about my heart's refusal to participate in that war. I'm not naïve enough to think that this was unjust or unfair. It was what it was. I'm simply saying that the draft board, as a social group, was simply not set up for this kind of heart-directed communication. The agreement in place for the friends of mine who did go to Vietnam was that if you were drafted, you went there whether you agreed with the war or not. The price I paid for disagreeing was being exiled from my country.

Today, there are millions of teenagers trapped in high schools that make absolutely no sense to them. The educational system is not relevant to who they are or what they truly want. There is no alternative to school for a fourteen-year-old student who consciously or subconsciously longs for something more meaningful. And at that age, truancy is a crime. There is a price to pay if these kids want to follow their hearts in relationship to education. In both cases, neither the draft board nor the school organize around Being Heart-Directed. They organize around the opposite—dictating the direction their members must follow.

I want to say again and again that I'm not speaking from any place of complaint. The school is as the school is, until enough people agree to make schools more heart-directed. The draft board in the United States has disappeared because people no longer agree to support the draft.

In summary, our Culture of Separation is what it is, to a large extent, because of the agreements we have with each other inside the groups that make it up. *But just as a culture has tremendous power over us through its agreements to avoid purpose, stillness, authenticity, connection, and heart-direction, we have tremendous power over the culture to change these old agreements into new ones that support Heart Awakening.* We can change them because they are *our* groups and *our* agreements—we're the ones making them! We just need to know what Heart Awakening agreements are.

Five Agreements that Transform Groups

If this book came with a sound track, you'd be hearing a dramatic drum roll right about now. The following sentence is the highlight and central focus of the entire book:

Just as we individually transform by deciding that we personally want to be more clear, present, real, connected, and heart-directed, so our social groups transform when we mutually decide that we want to be

more clear, present, real, connected and heart-directed with one another.
Our groups transform when we consciously and deliberately agree that
we want to use being in them as an opportunity to support one another
in Heart Awakening.

As soon as people within *any* group agree that they want to be more
Clear, Present, Real, Connected, and Heart-Directed with each other,
the qualities that arise from these Ways of Being start to weave themselves into that group culture. As the weaving progresses, the group is
launched into an entirely new social paradigm. It starts to realize and
manifest its unlimited capacity to accelerate Heart Awakening because
its members have agreed that they want this.

As the group recognizes its new capacity, its very nature changes.
Every group member now has better access to the practical and concrete
support needed to live into, to track, to practice, and to experiment with
being more fully awake with each other. The group becomes conscious
of itself as an awakening-friendly group. It begins to be an intentional
social container capable of holding the focus necessary for awakening.

Thus the Five Ways of Being can be turned into five powerful agreements we make with one another to consciously, intentionally and
radically create social environments that support Heart Awakening.
As such, they give us a practical way to change the existing Culture of
Separation from *within*, starting with our own families, friendships,
schools, and other groups.

If I could enlarge these four paragraphs you just read into fifty-foot-
tall sentences and place them in the collective mind like the Hollywood
sign overlooking Los Angeles, it would better convey my sense of how
important they are. I'm also aware that you may not be jumping up
and down in excitement quite yet, so I want to continue in hope that,
by the end of the chapter, you will be.

In all their elegant simplicity, the Five Ways of Being are translated
into questions, inquiries, and, ultimately, into consensus agreements

that have the power to transform our social groups and relationships. I call them the Five Ways of Being Together Agreements:

- Being Clear Together: Do we agree that we want to support each other's exploration of purpose?

- Being Present Together: Do we want more stillness with one another?

- Being Real Together: Do we want to be more spontaneous and authentic together?

- Being Connected Together: Do we want to intentionally practice giving and receiving love?

- Being Heart-Directed Together: Do we want to support one another in finding and following what we want?

Bringing these agreements into our relationships has a radical effect on them. When we collectively inquire, and then provide plenty of space over time for each person to answer sincerely and honestly, the ongoing conversation itself acts as a binding agent that helps create group coherence. For example, we become more real together just by asking the question, "Do we agree that we want to be more real together?"

As we sustain these agreements, trust grows. Defenses are lowered. Whenever one person has the wherewithal to be more Clear, Present, Real, Connected, and Heart-Directed, his or her willingness tends to bring forth that same willingness in others. People relax together because they're not wasting energy on pretense and defense. Also, just asking one another if we want to be Clear, Present, Real, Connected, and Heart-Directed together wildly increases the chances that we will be. The question itself has the capacity to set in motion its own fulfillment.

A question I often ask at the beginning of my Heart Circle workshops is whether or not people want to feel more connected to one another by the end of the workshop. A man attended one of these workshops, who, when asked this question, was clear that he didn't want to connect with anyone. I was a little surprised, given that connection is a major component of Heart Circle, but I recognized that he was being honest. As it turned out, instead of his preference having a negative impact on the other participants, it had the opposite effect. It helped everyone relax, knowing they could show up authentically, themselves. They felt equally as free to avoid him as he felt in avoiding them. This is exactly what happened. No one spoke to him all day. Ironically, I think he felt more connected to the group by the end of the workshop because everyone had honored what he wanted. I still don't know why he came, but I'm glad he did.

Before going into more detail about the power of this kind of group inquiry, I want to emphasize that making these agreements is not agreeing that we *will* be Clear, Present, Real, Connected, and Heart-Directed with one another. We're simply saying that we *want* to be these ways with one another. The difference is significant. Committing to be a certain way, such as agreeing we *will* be real with one another, takes away our freedom to be how we actually *are* in any given moment. This is visible in many religious and New Age groups. People commit to being positive and smiley, regardless of how they are feeling. Agreeing that we *want* to be Clear, Present, Real, Connected, and Heart-Directed is enough.

These agreements change everything! Let's examine in more detail how they work.

Being Clear Together

When we create the opportunity to freely talk about our purpose within any group we're in, there will obviously be a greater chance of finding out if everyone's personal purpose for being in the group is aligned with the group purpose. Is everyone in the right group? For example, this inquiry into purpose is now being played out in millions of marriages either consciously or unconsciously all around the world.

One of the partners begins to awaken and wants their marriage purpose to be about "awakening together." The other person may not know what awakening means. It may not be their time to awaken. That partner will often feel criticized when the other keeps asking for him or her to be more present, still, or connected. This requires a willingness for both partners to go deeply into the questions "What is the purpose of our marriage right now? Are we in the right relationship?" The more conscious the inquiry is between the partners, the less chance they will act out their differences with one another through conflict and power plays.

As another example, everyone within a business may agree that its purpose is to generate profit for owners, employees, or investors. But looking more deeply into purpose will bring up the question of *how* we are generating profit. Is our purpose to provide services or goods that increase the well-being of everyone involved? Or is mutual well-being not part of the purpose? Selling sugar-coated cereal may generate more profit than plain cereal, but is that sugar good for those eating it? A landscaping company may provide a weed-free yard to its customers, but does it protect the employees spraying the weed killer as well as the homeowners?

In general, a group becomes more powerful and effective whenever group members are clear and in agreement about:

- The purpose of the group
- The purpose each member has for being in the group
- The ultimate purpose of all groups

Relative to the first two bullet points, the more alignment there is between the group purpose and each member's purpose for being in the group, the greater the chance for cooperative success and mutual benefit.

As for the third bullet point, I'm suggesting that if we agree that the ultimate purpose of life is to come into love and connection, it may follow that the ultimate purpose of any group is to support its members coming into love and connection *with one another*. If a group is aware of this third level of purpose, it enters into an entirely new paradigm of possibility. Kindness, caring, and consideration become intrinsic parts of that group's culture. The group becomes a joy to be in. Fulfilling the personal and collective purposes of the group can then usually happen with greater ease.

When looking at groups likes armies or gangs, it may seem silly to suggest that love is the ultimate purpose of all groups. But consider the 17th Century Sikh warrior, Guru Gobind Singh. He is said to have used gold-infused arrowheads in war against Aurangzeb, his genocidal foe. He wanted the families of any opponents killed in battle to be provided for when the head of household didn't return home alive.

Likewise, telling an outlaw motorcycle gang that their purpose is "love" would probably lead to being smacked in the head with a tire iron. At the same time, loyalty to one another is their most fundamental agreement. Members are usually much more willing to sacrifice their lives for each other than are members of other social groups.

Any group will begin to radically transform when its members realize that the ultimate purpose for being together is to support one another's awakening into love.

Being Present Together

Groups truly thrive when members are present and still with one another, rather than being caught in their own individual stories, constant thinking, social conditioning, plotting, planning, and continuous doing. When stillness is valued, there is a much greater chance that the group will be transformative and enjoyable, rather than dysfunctional and boring. Just as coming out of constant thinking into stillness is a requirement for personal awakening, groups also need stillness and periods of silence in order for them to support awakening. Stillness is the footpath into presence. When people are present and their busy minds slow down, it's easier to listen to one another. As fewer words are used, more is communicated. Space is created for the original idea to emerge.

In stillness, people who typically dominate the group have a greater chance to sit back and allow others to be heard. Those who are used to sitting back have more opportunity to come forward. In silence, everyone has greater access to their inner wisdom. Children have a greater chance of being heard when adults are still. When children feel heard, they get still themselves. They don't have to use distraction to get attention when they already have the attention they need.

When there is group silence, there's greater opportunity for people to connect with themselves and one another *before* taking action as a group. Most group members in the Culture of Separation subconsciously try to connect by doing things together. In the Culture of Connection, group members consciously connect with one another and *then* decide what they want to do. Whoever came up with the phrase, "Ready, fire, aim!" must have known this.

When stillness is incorporated into a group's culture, Being Present is valued over being clever. People don't have to come up with the next witty thing in order to feel like they belong. Everyone has a better chance to relax and show up as they are.

More than anything else, when a group drops into stillness together, it gives people permission to be still in their other groups and relationships. Silence and stillness have a chance to spread. This isn't a disconnected, awkward silence in which people run out of things to say. It's the kind of silence where eye contact is used to communicate what words can't. In this small way, we can help calm the revved-up culture we live in.

As group members encourage one another to be more present, ways for stillness to manifest will surface organically within the group. One group may decide to begin and end its meetings with a minute or two of silence. In another group, members may agree to create more contemplative stillness before the next person speaks. A family may carve out more home time where there is no music, cell phone, computer, TV, or electrical interference.

Being Real Together

When we gather in any social setting, we bring our emotions with us. Some of our emotions will be open for everyone to see, but most will be hidden, either intentionally or unintentionally. To a large degree, a group is functional or dysfunctional according to how everyone's emotional life plays out within the collective environment of that group.

The Culture of Separation remains emotionally repressed through a hidden conspiracy that all of us embrace to one degree or another. But there is good news here. A conspiracy is simply an agreement to conspire! Because this is just an agreement, we can always agree to something else. We can agree that we want to create social environments that support emotional honesty and expression. We can agree to be real with one another. We can agree to use being together as an opportunity to care about and track what other group members are feeling.

Without a group agreement to be real, hidden agendas are more likely to create havoc. Third party talk becomes the norm. People talk *around* what they are feeling, rather than being direct. Roles replace presence. Pretending and pretension team up to squash the delight and ease of simply being who we are with one another.

What I am suggesting is simple, and anything but easy. Just bringing up the question of whether or not we want to be real can elicit angry, defensive responses such as, "Are you saying I'm not being real?" or, "If we do what you're calling being real, we'll get nothing done." The hardest reaction to counter, however, is the awkward silence this question can bring. Many people will be too terrified by the thought of being intentionally real with one another to say yes or no.

Even if the conversation does happen, and people do agree they want to be more authentic, the complexity of emotion and interaction comes into play. There is no playbook for this. But more good news: life is a self-correcting process that uses trial and error as its primary game plan. Reality itself knows the way. The agreement to be real opens the exploration into what being real actually means to every individual in the group.

Being Connected Together

We are already connected to one another, whether we directly experience this connection or not. Thus, there's nothing we have to do to connect. There is, however, something to undo. When we are with another person, we have the opportunity to undo our conditioned fear around the intimacy that comes with giving and receiving love. In some primal way, we are back on the school playground as five-year-olds. One comes up to the other and asks, "Do you want to be my friend?" Whether the answer is yes or no doesn't matter as much as the freedom those five-year-olds have in asking. As adults, we can create enough safety within our social groups to ask others if they want to connect more deeply.

Being Heart-Directed Together

The very heart of any group is opened when members support or hold space for one another to find out what each person wants from being in the group overall, and from moment to moment. When the focus is on what each person wants, rather than on what the group wants from each person, that group has a far greater chance to come alive and flourish.

All successful human interaction revolves around the simple act of two human beings reciprocally *feeling*, and then *caring about*, their own and each other's wants. Communities are successful to the degree to which this common caring occurs.

I know of a dental practice that employs two dentists, a hygienist, and an office manager. All four people understand that the success of their office depends, in part, on the strength of the connections they have with each other. Therefore, they make it a priority to meet once a week to find out what each person wants in order to make working together a better experience for them and their patients. If there are tensions, space is given to find out what each person is feeling and wanting. There is also space to talk about what each of them personally wants for making the office run more smoothly. They affectionately call these weekly meetings "office flossing."

Summary with a Catch

- When group members agree that they want the purpose of their being together to include Heart Awakening, their group becomes more vital and creative.

- When group members agree that they want more stillness within their group field, they become more present, creative, and attuned to one another.

- When members agree that they want to be real, they have a much better chance of bonding.

- When time and attention are devoted to members connecting with each other, differences are easier to bridge.

- When group members agree to support each other in discovering what they personally want by being in the group, a synergistic explosion of possibility occurs.

Applying these elemental Ways of Being Together is what we have been evolving towards since the first family clan gathered around the fire so many years ago. We have simply reached the point in our evolution to do this with greater intentionality and mutual agreement. We are moving towards true, heart-based community. We are moving into the Culture of Connection.

Identifying these five social agreements, and understanding their potential for rapid evolutionary transformation, is of immense value. The fully functional, truly sane group is, itself, part of a vast new frontier opening up as we proceed into the Twenty-first Century. We have barely scratched the surface of what relationships and groups can be when they are operating with members feeling connected to one another, where the collective wisdom of the group supports each member's sovereignty and creativity at the same time the group fulfills whatever purpose it has. The group that supports its members to be Clear, Present, Real, Connected, and Heart-Directed makes those members stronger. This in turn strengthens the group, which makes the individuals stronger, which strengthens the group. It's an upward spiral with no end.

Just as the Five Ways of Being provide individuals with a reliable, non-prescriptive, non-directing way of understanding and living into their own Heart Awakening, these same Five Ways of Being Together provide an equally powerful, living blueprint for how any group can transform into a social environment that supports Heart Awakening.

This summary about agreements takes us to the next obvious question: How do we actually introduce them into our existing groups—our families, friendships, schools, businesses, and organizations?

Here is where all of the fantastic good news about our culture-changing agreements runs into a bit of a snag! For most people, it is difficult to even know where to start. Do we get our families together some evening and announce that we have discovered these powerful agreements and then ask, "Who wants to play?" Do we excitedly tell our boss that we know how to bring the company into greater connection and vitality? Introducing, applying, and sustaining these agreements in any group is as challenging as kayaking through Class V river rapids. If you don't know what Class V rapids are, they're the ones you look at and say, "No way! Let's portage around them!"

For groups to transform, there has to be a clear and reliable process for bringing our new awakening-friendly agreements into them. The group container must be strong, and someone has to know what they're doing.

This takes us paddling right into Chapter 10. Tighten your life vest; hold onto your paddle, and follow the current. We're going to look at why being in any group or primary relationship is difficult, and why introducing these agreements to others is next to impossible without an effective process through which to do it.

WHERE MY LONGING BELONGS

It doesn't get better than this:
Finding the stillness beneath my mind
That splashes color
And peace
And sweet music
All over everything.

But why is this journey to stillness so hard?
Why the false turns
The twisted maybes
The bliss one minute and hell the next?

I just want to stay here
Right here
Right now
Where my longing belongs.

I know that nothing remains the same
That birds don't nest in the North when it's cold
That the East can't hold the sun past noon
That the world keeps spinning away from the West
That the South doesn't get along with Time.

But I don't care about any of that.
I just want to stay here
Right here
Right now
Where my longing belongs.

I want my mind
To fall in love with my heart
Like I did with Mary Lupher
On the first day of seventh grade.

I want my endless doubts and questions
To seem as silly to me
As the drunk guy seems
Standing in the middle of the street
Naked
Confused
Wondering how the hell he got there.

I want all my opinions about everything
To be reversed, cleaned, and cleared
Like my torn T-shirt is
When I fetch it
From the still-warm dryer
Down in the basement.

I just want to stay here
Right here
Right now
Where my longing belongs.

Bats return to their cave at dawn
To sleep upside down in the dark
And quietly smile
At all of us
Who think we know anything
About direction and light.

10

THE DIFFICULTY OF BEING IN GROUPS

Adopted Son

Sometimes a life wound is buried within us so deeply that it takes being with a close group of people for years before there's enough trust and bonding for the wound to surface and heal with that group's support. That a Heart Circle can continue for years is one of its irreplaceable elements. There is a kind of trust between people that only a prolonged history together creates.

In one Heart Circle I facilitated, a man told us during our first Circle check-in that he had been adopted at birth. I asked him if he had ever met his birth parents. He said he hadn't. When I asked whether he wanted to, he said he had no interest in that at all. I remembered thinking at the time, "Not true," but we didn't have enough history together for me to say anything other than "Oh!" Over the next few months, I frequently returned to the inquiry of whether he wanted to meet his birth parents, by asking things like: "Do you know where you were born? Do you suppose your dad had your warm smile? What do you think would happen if you did meet your mom and dad?"

Fast forward one year. Out of the blue, this adopted son blurted out during another check-in that he'd had a realization the night before. He said he was afraid that if he met his parents they would not want to see him again after the initial meeting. His original wound had surfaced—rejection at birth.

In the following weekly Heart Circles, he took space to explore how much he wanted to meet his parents. The entire Circle supported him in following his desire.

At this point if you—like all of us in the Circle back then—are looking for a happily-ever-after story, please brace yourself for disappointment. It didn't quite work out like that. Still, great healing took place for this man.

After months of exhaustive research, he finally found his birth mother. His biological father, a lifetime alcoholic, was no longer alive. His mother was dying of cancer and had six months to live. She lived in a poor rural community, while he had been raised by his adopted parents in an upper middle class home.

Their reunion came with a series of twists and surprises, some quite difficult for him to digest. One twist was particularly strange. He found out that he was the product of a one-night stand between his birth parents. One year later, that one-night stand was followed by an additional single night of passion between his father and mother. This second night produced another son. Rather than giving *this* son for adoption, the woman kept and raised him as a single mother. She didn't see the father again after that second night.

The younger brother hadn't been informed that he had an older brother until a week before the two brothers met. Understandably, he felt betrayed and angry that his mother hadn't told him.

An additional crazy twist in this family story was that both brothers ended up having the same first name. The mother unknowingly chose the same name for her second son that her first son had received from his adoptive parents.

It took the following year in Circle for this adopted man to assimilate what he experienced with his birth family, which included his mother's subsequent death and his younger brother's refusal to have contact with him. During this time, he often spoke about how grateful he was to have a Circle of people who supported him as he unearthed his past. He appreciated that we never tried to advise or fix him, but rather provided him with space to find what he wanted in relationship to his origins. He said that the bonding he had hoped to find with his birth family he found with us.

Daunting Difficulties

In Chapter 9, I talked about the power of bringing the Five Ways of Being Together Agreements into any group. Again, I can't overstate the potentially revolutionary impact of doing so. At the same time, thinking that all we have to do to transform our social groups is to make these agreements together is similar to thinking all we have to do to attain world peace is love one another. While both statements are true, they require a practical process through which we can do this.

In this chapter, I will become the *Speaker for the Difficulty*. I'll talk about the challenges that keep any group from being harmonious and effective. And again, I want to point out that even though these difficulties are something we're all confronted with daily, our Culture of Separation offers virtually no guidance for dealing with them. *It doesn't even acknowledge that these difficulties exist.*

After being *Speaker for the Difficulty* in this chapter, I'll switch hats in Chapter 11 and share a practical way to overcome the following difficulties:

- Difficulty One: Different Levels of Awareness
- Difficulty Two: It's Not an Intellectual Process
- Difficulty Three: Intimacy Avoidance Techniques

- Difficulty Four: Personality Disorders
- Difficulty Five: Emotional Pain and Trauma
- Difficulty Six: Conflicts and Differences
- Difficulty Seven: Someone Must Initially Facilitate

Difficulty One: Different Levels of Awareness

I'm not being cynical when I say that members of most social groups in our current Culture of Separation have little interest in personal awakening. They may have no frame of reference for what it means to watch their thoughts, feel their emotions, intentionally open to love, or follow what they truly want. Without a framework, getting members of any group to successfully sit together and talk about purpose, presence, emotions, love, and heart-direction is unlikely to happen. Not only may there be wide variation in interest levels, but the self-reflection these Five Ways of Being requires can activate our deepest fears around being open with one another.

Most groups in our current mass culture are organized around a functional purpose, and members often stay busy to avoid simply being. There are voices within these groups that don't recognize the value of any Heart-Awakening process when there is work to be done. In most families, there is that uncle or teenager who just rolls his eyes when asked if he wants to go deeper into family connection. "Uh…no, thanks." At school, there will be the conservative principle who says, "We're preparing our kids for four years of college, not for a night in a California hot tub." And if you suggest bringing Heart Awakening agreements into your local prison, the superintendent will probably confuse you with a dog dressed up in a tux, speaking in tongues. We need practical ways to bring these agreements into groups, while respecting those who want nothing to do with them.

There are millions of people in some phase of their awakening who will whole-heartedly welcome the introduction of the Five Ways of

Being Together into their relationships. But even when every member of a family or organization is interested in these transformational agreements, we still need a specific process for people to sustain their focus on them over time.

Difficulty Two: It's Not an Intellectual Process

Bringing these agreements into a group is not the same as goal setting, creating mission statements, or planning. Those are generally mind-centered activities that often have little real impact on the actual relationships between people within a group. In contrast, transforming a group culture through inquiry and the Five Ways of Being is a long, ongoing process. Patience is required. Heart-centered inquiries and agreements are to be lived into and experimented with from moment to moment. People must have ongoing, direct experiences of how these agreements work rather than a day's worth of mind-centered conversation.

Difficulty Three: Intimacy Avoidance Techniques

All of us have at our disposal certain standard tactics we unconsciously use to diminish the vitality and intimacy of our day-to-day interactions with others. We are doing nothing wrong when we use them. We're simply avoiding intimacy and connection. The primary reason for avoidance is a good one. We often associate intimacy and connection with pain and trauma, rather than with pleasure and well-being. Somewhere in our past, we may have experienced that staying open to others wasn't safe. We can use one or more of the following disconnection techniques to protect ourselves from disturbing our intimacy defenses:

Time Taking: When we consistently take up far more time and energy in our interactions with others than we give back. When we keep directing the flow of conversation back to ourselves.

Response Holding: When we hold back our authentic response to what is happening in our interactions. For example, when we are hurt by someone's words but say nothing to the person who said them.

Intellectualizing: When we consistently talk only about what we think and believe, rather than what we want and feel. One form of this is to talk endlessly without coming to any point or conclusion.

Story Telling: When we focus on events or the history of what has happened, rather than on what we feel or what we want in response to those events. For example, we may talk on and on about being left by a partner without showing the pain of our loss, or without getting in touch with what we want to either attract the partner back to us or move on.

Fixing: When we consistently offer solutions in response to what others are sharing, rather than just listening compassionately. For example, someone says they are sad and we immediately start suggesting ways for them to be happy.

Bubble Bursting: When what is happening in a social interaction reaches a high level of intimacy or intensity, and we feel compelled to redirect the focus away from that intimacy. For example, in a profound moment of silence after something important is shared, we crack a joke to break the silence.

Dissonance: When we go against what is happening in a social interaction by criticizing it, by being oppositional to what is happening, or by feigning confusion. An example of this is when someone speaks extensively and critically about what's happening within a group without saying what he or she personally wants to help the group function better.

Aloofness: When we're distant and choose not to share until prodded. This is different from being shy. For example, we may withdraw and act secretively to draw others in, but then, when given an opportunity to speak, we remain vague and distant.

Difficulty Four: Personality Disorders

If I left out this puzzle piece about personality disorders, we would end up with the la-la-la version of transformational group dynamics. It would result in a picture puzzle with a gaping hole through which you could see my own unwillingness to be real.

The intimacy avoidance strategies listed above are common and usually benign. In some way, we all use them. Dealing with people who have personality disorders, in a group or in a partnership, is an entirely different thing. In our Culture of Separation, personality disorders present a challenge that arises with alarming frequency in our marriages, families, friendships, businesses, schools, governments, and all forms of social gathering.

When I speak of people with personality disorders, I want to first say that my intent is to approach this topic with a great deal of respect. These people are us. They are not "crazy." They are in most ways as normal as anyone else. They have often survived a great deal of childhood trauma and deserve to be recognized and honored for their courage and strength as survivors.

They can also wreak havoc in any group, either in a heartbeat or over a long period of time, whichever comes first. People with these disorders can make it almost impossible for a group to come into functional resonance together because their own disorder tends to create disorder within any group or relationship in which there're involved.

I'm not a therapist. I'm not speaking clinically. I am speaking practically. Given the thousands of groups I have either facilitated or participated in, I'm aware that we all have some emotional wounding. Dealing with those wounds is a very real part of any group dynamic. Dealing with personality disorders presents a much more extreme challenge. By personality disorder, I'm *not* generally referring to people who have been clinically diagnosed as having a disorder. I'm referring primarily to people who have strong tendencies towards being narcissistic, psychopathic, or borderline but who are, at the same time, often highly functional and adaptive.

Defining these disorders is not part of my purpose here. You can explore these terms on your own as you wish. I simply want to use a broad brushstroke in drawing attention to the powerful effect people with such disorders can have on a group. In my experience, there are several reasons they can be so difficult.

The first reason is that people with these wounds are often highly functional, intelligent, charming, and even charismatic. This can make their dysfunction invisible until it shows up over time as control, manipulation, unpredictability, projected anger and blaming, lack of empathy, or being highly passive-aggressive.

The second difficulty is that our Culture of Separation has normalized these disorders. It often rewards narcissists and psychopaths with prestige, wealth, and power. Many national leaders, company CEOs, and abusive spouses are in positions of power and control, without any diagnostic recognition of their disorders. It is not unusual for psychopaths and narcissists to be running our companies, governments, places of worship, and armies. Some of the world's largest corporations profit from products or services that harm the consumer or environment. Creating cigarette ad campaigns for children, selling news that hypnotizes viewers with violence, and telling lies to start a war are all psychopathic acts.

Psychopathic tendencies and behaviors have often been so normalized that we feel powerless to do anything about them. People with these tendencies usually have little awareness of how they affect others, and rarely are they interested in self-reflection. Without introspection, there is little personal accountability. These folks are often "loose cannons" within group settings.

People with personality disorders generally require a disproportionate amount of the group's attention. There is often a vampire-like quality to the way they function in groups and relationships. They tend to siphon off the energy of others for themselves. They can be extremely good at this.

Most of us have no training in how to deal with these disorders. Not only are we not therapists, and thus unable to deal with this on a one-on-one basis, we are also not given the fundamental tools for how to effectively work with them in a group setting.

Recognizing these disorders, and the behavior that comes with them, is our first line of defense. People are effective in siphoning off group energy only if others can't see what they're actually doing. They use charm, personality, power, and lies to keep from being seen. We can't spiritually "transcend" the dysfunctional realities that come with these kinds of behavior. It only encourages the behavior to continue. This is a tough one, folks.

Difficulty Five: Emotional Pain and Trauma

> *As long as you are unable to access the power of the Now, every emotional pain that you experience leaves behind a residue of pain that lives on in you. It merges with the pain of the past, which was already there, and becomes lodged in your mind and body. This, of course, includes the pain you suffered as a child, caused by the unconsciousness of the world into which you were born.* —ECKHART TOLLE: *The Power of Now*

As most people know who have been in long-term committed relationships, the closer you get to someone, the more likely your "stuff" will come up. When people in any group start feeling trust and connection with others in the group, they will often—even if unconsciously—feel the safety to "be themselves." This means they will allow their pain bodies to surface and find expression. Knowing how to deal with this kind of emotional pain, shadow material, and hidden trauma in a group setting can be quite tricky. Group members have to learn how to "hold space" for one another as this occurs. Holding space means staying present when someone is in pain and avoiding the urge to fix or counsel them. In terms of group dynamic difficulties, this is somewhere near the top of the list.

Difficulty Six: Conflicts and Differences

You may find it hard to believe, but with all the difficulties of intimacy avoidance, varying levels of awareness, personality disorders, etc., it's possible that some group members may come into conflict with one another. For any social group to be truly successful, it must have effective ways to handle conflict and differences. And yet few people have any education in group conflict resolution or diversity training. Added to this, in our current mass culture, our use of social media has made it easier to avoid any kind of face to face conflict in real time. Thus, when conflict arises, members are tempted to say, "I don't need this. I'm out of here!" Without ways to deal with conflict and differences, our groups either fall apart quickly or die a slow death of complacency.

Difficulty Seven: Someone Must Initially Facilitate

For a group to become awakening-friendly, at least one member must be committed to the awakening process in themselves, and must be Clear, Present, Real, Connected, and Heart-Directed enough to deal with all of the difficulties listed above. Then, because a practical process is needed, that person has to understand how this practical process works, and be able to communicate how it works to others. In addition, that person must be able to deal with the complex dynamics of the group until others are ready to share this responsibility. Finally, to add one more touch of difficulty, that same someone has to be able to facilitate while at the same time fully participate as a group member. They can't hide in the role of facilitator. They must be able to go in and out of "facilitator mode" as needed.

Now that you've heard from the *Speaker for the Difficulty*, how do you feel about transforming your social groups—excited or discouraged? In either case, there *is* a way to successfully navigate through all of this, an effective way to deal with each one of these daunting difficulties.

I call it *Heart Circle*.

My Heart-Mind Re-Union

Talking out loud
And passionately to myself
My Lion-Heart says to my Lion-Mind:

"Oh, King of the Beasts
Symbol of freedom
Most glorious cat
What are you doing in this damn zoo?
You don't belong here.
This stinking concrete pen
Where you walk
Back and forth
Day after day
Is no home for any creature
But especially not for you.

Look at you!
A king in a cage
A captive in the commons
Shamefully imprisoned
On display
An object to fill up the vacant stares
Of nature-starved people
Who walk their children around the zoo
On a leash.

How'd you end up here, anyway?
Get caught in thought?
Forget who you were?
Or maybe you figured
It would be fun to be fed
Instead of stalking your own prey.
So, what's your game plan, Lion King?"

Still talking out loud
And passionately to myself
Now tinged with anger and sarcasm
My Lion-Mind says back to my Lion-Heart:

"Oh! So, there you are!
Nice of you to show up
After all these awful years
Which by the way
Have seemed like lifetimes to me.

What could possibly
Have taken you so long to get here?
And how did you think
That I was going to find my way out
Of this particularly dank
And dismal cage
Without *you*?

You are my Heart!
You are my Roar!
You're the embodiment of me!

It was you who disappeared
When I got trapped
Imprisoned in thought
Like everyone else in the forest
As it was cut down
Plundered and sold.
All of us suffered
All of us casualties of progress
Put in one kind of cage
Or another.

Lion King, my ass!
What did you expect me to do
With you
My own heart
Off hiding somewhere
Inaccessible
Spaced out in another world
All this time?

What could I do
But pace back and forth
Back and forth
Back and forth
Until your return?

I may be a lion
But I couldn't hurry grace.

At the same time
I can't tell you
How great it is to see you!
To be with my own heart again
To remember my roar
And feel the power of my body.
I feel a million times better already.
With you finally back
We can do anything together.

Let's get out of here!"

11

HEART CIRCLE DESIGN

The Brothers' Heart Circle Story

Most kids love Heart Circle. They love its simplicity, and the chance to speak and be spoken to as equals rather than being spoken down to by the big people. They also love the timeless ritual of simply sitting together in a circle.

Many years ago, I facilitated a Heart Circle training in Sydney, Australia. I stayed in the home of Andrew, my host, who was a single father with three boys, twins aged five and a seven-year-old. When one of these boys asked me why I was in his house, I told him about Heart Circle. All three spontaneously said they wanted to be in a Heart Circle, too.

That night before bed, the five of us sat cross-legged on their bedroom floor in Circle. I briefly went through the Heart Circle steps. Then we lit a candle, placed it in the center of the Circle, held hands, and sat still together. These were active little boys who previously couldn't sit still for more than thirty seconds at a time. But that night, no one moved or opened their eyes for a full five minutes.

To check in, each of us said a few words to describe what we were feeling. Luc, one of the twins, took the lead, blurting out that he was angry because his older brother, Mathew had hit him before the Circle began. To their father's surprise, Mathew said, "Sorry, Luc, I won't do it again." While that may not be the absolute truth for Mathew, it was true for him in that moment and we knew he was being sincere.

After we had all checked in, we gave each other some appreciative feedback and then took turns holding space for each other about what we wanted.

I don't remember what any of us said that night, but I do remember the impact the Circle had on Andrew. He told me later that he rarely asked his boys what they wanted. Instead, he was constantly telling them what to do. That night, we closed in silence like we had begun—holding hands, eyes shut, basking in the sweet, resonant field between us. I sensed that this was a first-time experience for these four family members.

The next night, after a full day of Heart Circle training in Sidney, I came back to Andrew's home and immediately lay down to rest, tired from the day's output of energy. Thirty minutes later, Andrew knocked on my door and said his boys were requesting my presence. I got up, went with him to their room, and there they were: quietly sitting cross-legged, with an unlit candle in the center of the room, waiting for the five of us to start Heart Circle.

Ask me why I love the work I do.

Heart Circle Elements

I developed the Heart Circle slowly over the many years I've been facilitating circles. I didn't sit down and say, "I think I'll come up with a social process that supports Heart Awakening." Instead, I paid attention to what was happening in circle after circle while being with people who shared a common desire to be more awake and aware in everyday life. As we sat together, I watched for patterns and common themes relating to individual awakening and building conscious community. I wanted to understand group dynamics clearly enough to build a strong foundation for circles that supported Heart Awakening.

Before I talk about what a Heart Circle is, I want to share some of the basic elements of its design so that you have a deeper understanding of why Heart Circles function the way they do. Even though the following elements may seem somewhat abstract, I think you'll enjoy how practical and simple they are:

- Social Containers
- The Pyramid and the Circle
- Do-Be Groups
- A Way Through Daunting Difficulties
- Matching Traditional Circle Format with The Five Ways of Being
- Transforming Existing Social Groups

Social Containers

A *physical* container, by definition, is made to hold or contain something. A trashcan holds trash and a shiny red box on Valentine's Day holds chocolates. A kitchen holds what's needed to prepare food. These are physical containers that hold physical objects.

There are also *social* containers. Marriage is a social container that holds people in primary relationship with one another. A softball league holds teams so players can play together. All social groups, such as businesses, schools, or governments, are containers that hold people together to contain the activities they were created to hold.

And there are more subtle containers—a verbal or written agreement between two people to lend or borrow money, for example. Such an agreement is a container that holds the intent of the people around the terms of that loan. A diet is a container that holds a person's intention to eat differently.

To understand groups, we have to recognize that they exist to contain something. That "something" includes, among many other things, each group member's purpose for being in the group. Groups help people hold their focus on their purpose or reasons for being in the group. It doesn't matter what the groups are. We're in them to be with other people who share a similar purpose, regardless of whether that group purpose is conscious or unconscious. Said another way, all groups exist to fulfill some purpose, and without that purpose, there would be no group because people would have no reason to be in the group. If we want to play a sport, we find people who want to play that sport with us. If we want friends, we find at least one person who wants to spend time with us. When a group no longer has a commonly shared purpose, it dissolves.

In designing Heart Circle, I was aware that the single most critical element within the design was to clearly identify its purpose for existing. *The primary purpose of Heart Circle is to give members a way to support one another in Heart Awakening.* It is to create an intentional social container in which people practice being Clear, Present, Real, Connected, and Heart-Directed together. Embedded within this purpose is the opportunity for people to change the mass culture agreements now in play—avoiding inquiry, staying in constant motion, hiding our emotions, downplaying connection and love, and following our social conditioning.

The Pyramid and the Circle

Groups are either organized hierarchically—where control of the group comes from a system of pyramidal ranking and decision-making—or they are organized non-hierarchically, so all the members are in control of what happens within the group. The military is a good example of a hierarchal pyramid. A group of friends is an example of a non-hierarchical circle.

Some groups have elements of both pyramid and circle, but are predominantly one or the other. For example, within a business, the owner may make the final decisions while encouraging employees to contribute to those decisions. On the other hand, a group of friends can be a circle that has a pyramidal feel because one person consistently leads while the others follow.

Some pyramidal groups can't function effectively as a circle, like the military or a prison. Some circle groups can't function effectively as a pyramid, like a marriage. Some patriarchic husbands or matriarchic wives may disagree with this, but I'm just saying …

Heart Circle must be organized as a circle rather than a pyramid. This allows each member to take full responsibility for the quality of group communication and connection. Decisions are made by consensus. The Circle is all-member-facilitated. These things are required for each Heart Circle member to experience and deal with the paradoxical relationship between their personal sovereignty and their connection to each other.

This will get clearer in the next chapter.

Do-Be Groups

There are two kinds of social groups: *Doing* groups and *Being* groups. Doing groups form around fulfilling a particular task or tasks, whereas Being groups form around members being together in community. A charitable organization is an example of a Doing group because it is formed around fulfilling a specific charitable function. A family is a Being group that has no particular task to fulfill, but is instead a community container within which family members live together in mutual support of one another. Ideally.

Groups can also incorporate both Doing and Being into their functions. While a church is a Being group, many task-oriented Doing groups can form within it, like community service committees. Similarly, a Doing group may configure itself into a Being group, as when business employees and employers get together during their annual holiday office party.

Groups can also be formed as hybrids, incorporating Being together and Doing as their combined purpose, which is different from simply adding doing or being into a few of their functions. For example, some Being groups come together in community by being involved in a common Doing activity. I'm part of a dance community in Ashland, Oregon. We free-form dance together two or three times a week. Dancing is something we *do* together but it's really our way of *being* together. This kind of hybrid social group lies between Doing and Being, as do amateur sports teams, reading clubs, birthday parties, and so forth.

People usually come into Doing groups with much less expectation around social intimacy and connection among the doers. There is a job to be done. There's a greater tendency to say, "Let's get busy with what we're here to do," even if there's tension in the room, or superficial talk, or people not actually knowing each other. Doing trumps Being.

People are in Being groups primarily *for* social intimacy and connection, whether their need for this is conscious or not. There is no compelling task at hand that necessarily keeps people from addressing that tension in the room, or getting to know one another better, or taking the conversation deeper.

This can get a little complex. In Being groups, like families, friendships, sports teams, or bridge clubs, many of the group members may cover up their fear of intimacy and connection by staying in constant Doing mode. Doing is their way of staying away from Being. These folks will be the ones who will be either cynical or skeptical of efforts to bring greater connection into the group. They simply won't want to play. While most of us have some trace of this resistance to social intimacy, in this case, I'm talking about those of us who are clear and adamant about not wanting closeness and connection.

A Heart Circle is a Being Group. It is not organized around members doing anything specific together, even though members can decide to do anything they want together. I'll explain this more fully in the next chapter. It's an essential element in understanding how Heart Circle works.

A Way Through Daunting Difficulties

I was keenly aware that for Heart Circle to be truly effective, it had to have ways for members to deal with the "daunting difficulties" outlined in the last chapter. Here is a brief summary of those difficulties and how Heart Circle deals with them:

Difficulty One: Different Levels of Awareness

Most members of most social groups in our current Culture of Separation have no frame of reference for what it means to watch their thoughts, to feel their emotions, to intentionally open to love, and to follow what they truly want. Without a framework, getting members of any group to successfully sit together and talk about purpose, presence, emotions, love, and heart-direction is unlikely to happen.

Heart Circle is organized around the Five Ways of Being. Its format encourages inquiry into purpose, presence, authenticity, connection, and heart direction. Because this organizational intent is so clear and stated so openly, people have a clear choice to be part of a Heart Circle based upon their interest in personal and group transformation. Thus people self-select their way into Circle. This minimizes or eliminates altogether the difficulty of being in a group or relationship in which members have little or no interest in Heart Awakening.

Difficulty Two: It's Not an Intellectual Process

People may confuse the Heart Circle process with planning and goal setting.

As soon as people are introduced to the format of Heart Circle, it will be obvious that it involves being heart-centered rather than mind-centered.

Difficulty Three: Intimacy Avoidance Techniques

All groups have to deal with the ways in which we avoid being real and present with one another while in a larger group.

The entire process of Heart Circle is designed to create a social environment that *welcomes* these avoidance techniques so that they can be identified, honored and disassembled. How about that?

Difficulty Four: Personality Disorders

People with personality disorders can wreak havoc within any group or relationship.

In the Heart Circle process, members are in Circle to consciously explore what they are feeling and wanting. People with personality disorders can only malfunction in a social environment when these two questions are hidden and unexplored. They will either leave the Circle or not join it in the first place unless they are ready to explore their own emotional wounding and hidden motives.

Difficulty Five: Emotional Pain and Trauma

Almost all us have some form of frozen emotional pain and trauma. It comes with being born into a mass culture that has not yet found its heart. Being in close committed relationships or community can thaw these wounds, allowing them to surface and heal. Knowing how to deal with this kind of pain when it does surface is essential for any group or relationship to function smoothly.

Heart Circles are formed with the intention that each member experiments with and develops his or her capacity to listen empathically and to be present with others. They provide an environment that supports people in consciously opening their hearts to one another. This helps Circle members avoid the understandable tendency to counsel, advise, or fix one another. In Heart Circle, loving presence and self-inquiry are the salve for emotional wounding. It's enough.

Difficulty Six: Conflict and Differences

Conflict and differences within groups or relationships are inevitable. Groups must have clear ways to resolve conflict, and to use differences so that they expand tolerance and diversity.

Heart Circle provides an environment in which members have an effective way of dealing with conflict and difference through the Five Ways of Being. The process doesn't need a scripted format or special facilitation. It allows members to see how conflict and differences can strengthen their bonds rather than weaken them.

Difficulty Seven: Transformational Group Dynamics Require Skilled Facilitation

Facilitating any group often takes immense skill and experience.

As I will explain in the next chapter, Heart Circles begin with just two people, rather than with a larger group. In pairs, people can experience the Heart Circle process without having to simultaneously deal with the complexity of group dynamics. When both people in this mini Heart Circle are ready, they can add new members one at a time. This approach increases the possibility for a successful Heart Circle to form by roughly a thousand times.

Matching Traditional Circle Format with The Five Ways of Being

When I first began studying circle dynamics in Toronto with Ross Laing, I was introduced to the traditional *wisdom circle*. The wisdom circle has been used within many cultures throughout the world for thousands of years. It is used for making consensual community decisions or to create community space for ceremony, prayer, and healing.

Since the 1960's, New Age culture has adopted parts of these circle traditions and created men's and women's circles, manifesting circles, healing groups, prayer circles, addiction rehabilitation meetings, spiritual study circles, community gatherings and social action teams. Circle wisdom sensibilities have also entered the mainstream culture and been utilized in processes such as town hall meetings and creative teams within businesses. Many NGO's and the United Nations use traditional circle principles in their ongoing work.

Most wisdom circles have a common format that includes five elements:

- Before entering "circle space," circle members get clear on why the circle is being called and what each person wants by being in it.

- With that clarity, the circle begins with "tuning in." Members use prayer, silence, invocation, or some ceremonial ritual that allows them to transition from their thoughts and activities outside of circle into the stillness of the present moment.

- Tuning in is followed by "checking in." Each member briefly shares what he or she is experiencing or wanting as the circle opens.

- Next, any member can receive the attention of the other circle members in order for that member to better speak from his or her heart about whatever the circle is about.

- When everyone who wants to speak has done so, and after any group decisions are made through consensus or elder wisdom, the circle *closes* with prayer, silence or simple ritual.

I use this format in my own circle facilitation work, but with one modification. After checking in, in Heart Circle there is an opportunity for circle members to briefly share appreciative feedback with one another. This addition came through the suggestion of Amina Knowlan, one of the best circle teachers I've met. She is the founder of Matrix Leadership Institute in Boulder, Colorado.

After my first decade of facilitating circles, I began to see patterns in relationship to what we are actually doing in circle. I saw that before beginning a circle, we needed to be *clear* about its purpose through our willingness to talk about it. I noticed we were getting *present* by tuning in. We were being *real* by checking in. Then we were getting *connected* by giving appreciative feedback to one another. And finally, by giving attention to what each person truly wanted to say, do, or inquire into while in the circle, we were being *heart-directed.*

Looking at this format, you may have noticed the Five Ways of Being. I certainly did. I recognized the perfect overlay between the circle format and these ways of being. Through their overlay, each simultaneously on top of the other, I saw how Heart Awakening could be defined by identifying these Five Ways of Being, and how useful this definition could be because it was a practical way to cut across all spiritual and religious ideas and practices.

As importantly, I also saw how the traditional circle format or agenda could provide a laboratory, classroom and community in which people could *practice* being Clear, Present, Real, Connected and Heart-Directed with each other and thus be given real support in Heart Awakening.

I saw even further that the circle was also a place to *experiment* and find out what happens when two or more people agree to organize around these awakening intentions. How much more quickly do we individually awaken with this kind of practical awakening support? What happens to the group itself when these agreements are in place? Can these Ways of Being be introduced to and sustained by any group? What possibilities open up for creative problem solving, remediating conflict, therapeutic healing, community building—when we connect with one another in these ways? In designing Heart Circle, I saw the opportunity for the exploration of all of this and much, much more.

More than anything else, I wanted Heart Circle to be a grand experiment and an awakening playground in which anyone who wished could bring their own experience, genius, perspective, and presence to a social environment that everyone involved would help create. I wanted each Circle member to become a conscious agent of individual, social, and evolutionary change as the experiment unfolded.

Transforming Existing Social Groups

The last essential element of the Heart Circle design is perhaps the most important. I wanted to create a process that could help transform our *existing social groups, so that we wouldn't be reliant only on specialized spiritual, religious, or self-help groups* to receive awakening support. Changing our *existing groups* can lead to exponential, collective, transformational growth because our families, friendships, schools, and businesses are the groups we spend the majority of our time in. They have the greatest influence on us, and some of them we remain in for a major portion of our lives. For me, transforming our existing groups is our greatest hope for addressing the vast array of planetary problems, which can only be resolved through a collective change in consciousness.

I hope you can sense the extraordinary significance of this.

Let's now take a look at what a Heart Circle actually is!

GETTING FREE

How do you free yourself
From the pain that you're in?

I'll tell you how.

Go find a Dragon Slayer
And ask for her sword.

Then with that blade in hand
Cut all of your fear
Into bite-size pieces
And feed them to your goat.

Goats can eat anything.

12

WHAT IS A HEART CIRCLE?

The Airport

In my own longstanding men's Heart Circle, one man shared something that permanently enriched my understanding of what Heart Circle can be. On this particular night, he checked in with the news that he had been at our nearby city airport the previous Monday morning, ready to go on a sales trip to New York. He said he was deeply depressed and that his depression had led to a panic attack. He didn't know if he could actually board the plane. He said it took him almost two hours of white-knuckling, but he did manage to board on time. He told us how grateful he was to be able to share his "weakness" so openly with us.

Another man in the Circle responded by asking why he hadn't reached out while he was at the airport. We didn't live that far away. One of us could have met him there in the terminal within ten minutes. This was before 9/11 and long security screening lines.

This led to an agreement that's still in place in our men's Circle today, twenty-two years later. We agreed that if any of us was ever in crisis, all we had to do was call one other member and say, "I'm at the airport." Nothing more. This would be our signal for one—or all—of us to drop whatever we were doing and get to where that brother was.

No questions asked, day or night. No matter where we are, we agree to show up for one another. We made this agreement a lifetime pledge. Four simple words—I'm at the airport—and we'll be there.

Although we have used this only one time in twenty-two years, that one time was important. And just as important as that event itself—we know we have each other covered. For life.

What is a Heart Circle?

Heart Circle is a specific kind of traditional wisdom circle. Ideally, it has between two and ten members. Circle meetings are weekly or bimonthly. The length of these meetings is anywhere from thirty minutes to two and a half hours. It is a Being Group that has no other functional purpose than to provide mutual support for its members to awaken. It also doesn't have any specific Doing functions associated with *how* to awaken, such as doing yoga or following any particular set of teachings. It stays neutral so that each Circle member is free to do or follow whatever awakening practices he or she wants. Circle can be made up of members from any existing social group or of people who have just met. It can be a circle of friends, a family circle, an organization or school circle, or a business circle. It can be made up of men only or women only, or it can be a mixed gender group.

Heart Circles are eventually all-member facilitated. Sometimes an experienced facilitator can start a group and then leave the facilitator position as members are ready to assume the responsibilities that come with that role. Heart Circles are *committed* circles rather than drop-in circles. Members commit to meeting with one another for a specific time period, initially for four to eight weeks. New members can then join, but only through consensus agreement by the original Circle members.

Heart Circle uses the following format, modified from traditional wisdom circle format, to give its members an opportunity to practice the Five Ways of Being with one another:

- Being Clear: Before starting a Heart Circle, members come into agreement that the purpose of being together is to support one another in Heart Awakening and in coming into closer connection, community and friendship with one another.

- Being Present: The actual Heart Circle begins with *tuning in* by using several minutes of silence so that members can quiet their minds, experience what they are feeling within their bodies, and become aware of the presence of the other group members.

- Being Real: After tuning in, members check in with one another by briefly sharing what they are experiencing emotionally in that moment.

- Being Connected: After checking in, members take another ten or so minutes to exchange appreciative feedback between each other. One member expresses to another member something he or she appreciates about that person, while the rest of the group listens in, until each member has either received or given this kind of heart-centered feedback.

- Being Heart-Directed: After sharing appreciative feedback, the bulk of the Heart Circle time is spent *holding space* for one another. Anyone can ask for the attention of the others in Circle. If everyone agrees to give their attention, that person can take five, ten, or more minutes in order to self-reflect or gain insight and clarity around any aspect of life he or she wants to examine. If people don't know what they want to focus on, they can use the attention to explore what their wants might be. Someone may want to look at an issue concerning partnership or parenting. Another may want to explore a health issue. It can be about anything. However, because of the agreed-upon purpose of the Heart Circle, it will ultimately relate to this question: What do I want in order to be more clear, present, real, connected, or heart-directed in my life? Anyone can receive attention as long as other members want to give their attention to him or her, and as long as there is time to do so before the Circle closes.

- Closure: Members sit in silence for a few minutes. They then take turns saying whether they are feeling *complete* or *incomplete* in relationship to their time in that particular gathering. If a member says he or she feels incomplete, the simple act of saying so serves as a kind of completion that allows the Circle to close gracefully.

I will be giving more detail about each of these steps in Chapter 14.

Advantages of Being in Heart Circle

Heart Circles are quite amazing, not because of what we *do* while we're in them, but because of what we can observe and consciously *experience* while in them. And what we observe and experience is our own life: our thought patterns, emotional responses, desires and beliefs, strengths and weaknesses, and insights as to how we relate to others. In Heart Circle, we receive a fractal reflection back to us of what is happening in ourselves, so we can adjust accordingly. This increased awareness gives us a growing sense of individual sovereignty, as well as greater sensitivity to our connection with others.

Within a Heart Circle, whatever comes up for individual members or for the group as a whole can be addressed directly and intentionally. It is a social space where individual members can explore their core issues, desires, goals, ambitions, and fears with support of the Circle in that exploration.

Below are other, more specific opportunities available in Heart Circle:

- Exploring the Fundamental Purpose of All Social Groups: In Heart Circle, we have a chance to *experience* that the ultimate purpose of family, community, and nation is to support one another in being more conscious, aware, loving human beings. The more we understand this, the more intentional we become in giving and receiving this fundamental support. The more we give and receive such support, the stronger and more vital our family, community, and nation become.

- Responding Authentically: In Heart Circle, we have ongoing opportunities to overcome any authoritarian conditioning telling us that showing up as we are is inappropriate, shameful, or forbidden. Whether we were exiled from our spontaneity in a classroom with our hand forever held up, or in a living room where our joy was never welcome, Heart Circle provides a place in which we can thaw our heart's frozen responses to life and to each other. We can practice giving our spontaneous, heartfelt responses to the people we're interacting with, as we encourage their being authentic with us.

- Identifying and Being Open about What We Want: In Heart Circle, we have an opportunity to directly experience that every social relationship is healthy, connective, and effective to the degree that everyone in it knows and cares about what each person wants from their interacting together. We have a chance to see that the more honest we are about what we want, and the more interested we are in what others want, the more likely it is that our interactions will be successful and fulfilling. Heart Circle provides support in finding our life gifts, and then in receiving support manifesting those gifts—gifts we *must* bring to life to feel whole and complete.

Because we are culturally bombarded by thousands of daily messages cleverly defining our needs, wants, goals, and desires for us, Heart Circle is a refuge from all of those messages. As each member finds and expresses his or her own sense of direction, it becomes possible for the Circle to support that direction—to augment, to suggest, but inherently to support each member's sovereign decisions.

- **Learning How to Intentionally Create Deep Friendships and Community:** One of the primary purposes for being in Heart Circle is to experience what is required to bond with others in the Circle, so we can bond with others more easily outside of Circle. The Five Ways of Being Together provide us with a blueprint for building community and strong friendships. We get a chance to directly experience what happens when we agree that we want to be Clear, Present, Real, Connected, and Heart-Directed with each other, and then support one another in holding our focus on these intentions.

- **Creating Social Safety Nets:** Heart Circle provides a place of mutual safety and support when there is crisis in our personal life or community. Crisis can show up in many forms. It can be financial, emotional, environmental, relational, or it can involve our health or the health of those we love. The Circle itself can provide refuge as members get to know, trust, and count on one another through meeting regularly over a sustained period of time. The Circle can also provide a template for creating this kind of social safety net in other groups, particularly in our families or close groups of friends.

- **A Place for Honesty and Self-Revealing:** Each Heart Circle meeting provides us with space to deal with our limitations, our hidden agendas and conditioning, our addictions, our self-defeating tendencies, our core-unworthiness, our failures, and our relational limitations. There is space provided for this kind of honesty because each member of the Circle is also exploring how to build an atmosphere of non-judgment and kindness. Heart Circle gives us access to constructive criticism, praise, and all forms of candid input from people who are committed to their own Heart Awakening. We can find out how our ideas, wants, and heartfelt desires might become more actualized through the contribution of others. It is a place to ask for and accept assistance.

- A Place for Humor, Celebration, Laughter, and Lightness of Being: In Heart Circle, one fundamental agreement between members, spoken and unspoken, is that we want to enjoy being with one another. The agreement is that we want to experience the greater reality that we are meant to enjoy life. It's a place to discover wonder inside the ordinary: to see the miraculous in each other, to relax together, and to celebrate life.

- A Place to Respond to the Social Issues of Our Times: *Heart Circles are not designed to be social action groups.* There are other groups with that intent. Heart Circle is designed to be a place to get in touch with what we are feeling *about these social issues.* It's also a place to explore how we want to respond to them. For example, climate change could well be the over-riding social issue that defines our times. Heart Circle provides a place for us to deal with the emotional and physical realities that come with the possible calamities awaiting us if the planet continues to warm.

- Heart Awakening: The very heart of Heart Circle is to provide each other with encouragement, focus, and support for making the grand, perceptual leap into Heart Awakening. Heart Circle begins and ends with this intent. This is personal to you. It is to support *your* leap into connection with everything: into the lap of Love. It's also about developing *your* capacity to support others in their Heart Awakening. It is this common intent that makes Heart Circle a Heart Circle.

Beginning a Heart Circle

In 2006, I wrote a book called *Heart Circles*. In 2009, I re-wrote it and re-named it *The Heart Circle Process*. For a self-published book, it sold well, and each year I watched the demand for it grow. Besides being available online and in some bookstores, I sold and used it as a teaching tool for my Heart Circle workshops.

In 2012, I stopped publishing this book. I had written it to show people how they could start and sustain their own Heart Circles. The reason I took it out of circulation was that, while I'd been telling people they could start and sustain their own Circles by following the process laid out in my book, I began to see over time that this wasn't actually true. Few Circles had succeeded without initial facilitation by me or another trained Heart Circle facilitator. I had to accept that teaching others how to deal with the massively complex dynamics of any group is not possible in the way I was suggesting it was. I couldn't continue selling it and be in my integrity. The company owners who printed *Heart Circle* thought I was nuts.

I decided to re-write my book for a third time, thinking it would only take a few months to make what I'd been promising more attainable. Several months turned into six years of writing and rewriting, thinking and rethinking, experimenting and re-experimenting. I needed those years to re-envision how Heart Circles can work without an experienced facilitator.

During this six-year process, I had two realizations about the new book. First, I needed to greatly expand my emphasis on the Five Ways of Being from what I wrote in the first two books. I have done that in this book so that it reflects my own love and respect for the simplicity and power of these five awakening elements.

My second realization was that I had to re-envision how a Heart Circle begins. While facilitating Heart Circles in the past, I often encouraged group members to pair up with one another in short, one-on-one, mini Heart Circles outside of the regular weekly or bimonthly group Circle. Pairing up was a way for members to deepen their connection with one another while at the same time deepening their understanding of how to tune in, check in, connect up, and hold space around what people truly wanted.

As people worked with these mini Circles, I saw how powerful they were. Members were connecting with each other in profound ways in these simple half-hour exchanges. They were also able to practice using the Heart Circle format without my facilitation. They got along just fine without me.

Finally, it dawned on me that these one-on-one Circles were the ideal way to start a Heart Circle. This realization had a major impact on my own understanding of circle dynamics. As I mentioned, the greatest advantage to starting a Heart Circle with just one other person is that it's possible to learn a great deal about relational dynamics without having to track the complex interactions of a larger group. This is similar to learning to drive. We don't begin by rushing into traffic on an eight-lane freeway. We begin by separating ourselves from traffic and getting to know the basic driving elements of steering, stopping, and starting. After these elements are mastered, it's then time to leave the empty parking lot and venture onto the road to frolic with the other cars.

Another advantage of starting a Heart Circle with just one other person is that we can be more certain the other person is sincere in wanting to explore personal and group transformation with us. We choose the person *because* we have already experienced that he or she wants this. We also choose someone because we like and trust him or her; we're both working with pre-existing resonance and trust. For example, if a family sits in Circle together, there may be deep-seated conflicts that surface as a result of everyone being more open and honest. Family system dynamics are extremely complex to traverse. Meeting with just one other family member who really wants to explore this process with you is infinitely easier and more fruitful than trying to initially meet with the larger family. Others can join in later as they sense the value of what the two of you are experiencing together.

There is another advantage of starting small. Again, using the car metaphor, one of the challenges of driving is dealing with drivers who tailgate, weave in and out of traffic, or drive while intoxicated. As I mentioned previously about personality disorders, there can be one person within a larger group who needs far more attention than the group can give. In pairs, this potential mismatch is greatly minimized.

Also, being with one other person is generally much more relaxing than being in a larger group. And if the one-on-one Circle doesn't work for either one of the pair, it's much easier to find another person who is a better fit. It's a little like five-minute speed dating. If the chemistry isn't there, we can clang the bell and move on.

Creating a larger Heart Circle is much easier after being in a one-on-one Circle because there are now two of you who are experiencing a deeper connection as a result of being in your own Circle together. In a group, it often takes at least four weeks for the group to "gel" and be in harmony. With two people, it's almost instantaneous. Starting as a pair also means that there will be two of you acting as a team to show those who join later how the Circle works. There will be two of you to hold space as deeper group issues surface. It will be easier to invite others into your Circle because both of you will be using the Five Ways of Being in daily life, and thus able to *model* these Ways of Being rather than simply *talk* about them.

My realization about beginning a Heart Circle with two people has led to an entirely different approach to how I now work with families and organizations. Instead of going *into* an existing social group to start a Heart Circle, I now invite members *out* of that group to start a Heart Circle. Then, after four weeks together, other members can be invited into the mini Circle, one at a time, once the initial members have a clear grasp of how the Heart Circle process works.

Where to Begin a Heart Circle

Heart Circles can be formed in any area of our social life, from friendships to families to organizations of all kinds. The possibilities are limitless.

Close Friendships

Existing friends make the best Heart Circle members! And a best friend is the best person to begin a Heart Circle with. It can grow into a larger Circle of friends after the two friends experience a Heart Circle together for the initial four or eight weeks.

Committed Partnerships

The primary reason to be together in a marriage or committed relationship is to support each other in becoming more present and real with each other, more heart-directed, and more in love. Since this is the same purpose as a Heart Circle, there is a natural marriage between Heart Circle and primary relationships. Spending an hour each week in Circle with your primary partner can dramatically enrich any union.

Families

A family is a Heart Circle. Weekly or bi-monthly family meetings can be formed to find out what each person in the family is feeling and wanting in order to be happier in the family.

Children, especially, love Circle because it resonates with their need for quality attention. Encouraging them to communicate directly gives them a sense of being an integral part of the family, regardless of their age. They are treated as sovereign beings who are participating in creating their own lives, rather than being caught up in the mindset of the larger Culture of Separation and all the dramas that come with it. Regular family Heart Circle increases family intimacy while serving as an antidote to living together without bonding together.

Men's and Women's Groups

Something happens when men are in Circle with other men and women are in Circle with other women. There is a power inherent in this that other cultures and civilizations often understood and utilized. You may want to explore forming a gender specific group to find out for yourself the value of a men's or women's Heart Circle.

If you are already in a men's or women's group, you may want to experiment with this Heart Circle process and adapt any part of it that serves your group.

Churches and Temples

A church or temple can increase the creativity and self-organizing capacity of its congregants by tenfold almost overnight by forming autonomous Heart Circles within the church. The Circle inverts the hierarchical structure of the church so that the paid staff and leadership end up doing ten percent of whatever is accomplished in the Circle while congregants contribute the other ninety percent, instead of the other way around. This is because Heart Circles are self-forming, self-facilitated, and self-activating.

Many churches and temples will agree with the Heart Circle purpose: to intentionally create an ongoing, enjoyable social environment that supports each person in becoming more present, real, connected, and heart-directed in life and with one another. It is a natural fit.

Businesses

It is common sense to say that when people within a business are allowed to work from their passion, rather than from just putting in time, and when everyone within the business is communicating more openly and honestly, the business will more likely flourish. With some modifications, Heart Circle within businesses can help accomplish this.

The caveat with businesses is that Heart Circle is rarely effective unless it occurs *outside* of the business. This is because businesses have a primary intent to generate income, whereas the primary intent in Heart Circle is to support one another in Heart Awakening. This is as it should be. The business is a container for its specific intention, and can't be mixed with a Heart Circle's very different intention. If you want to play soccer, you don't join a band. They are two different containers for two different purposes.

The other reason Heart Circle needs to be formed by business members outside of their business is because most businesses are hierarchically structured. People have hierarchical roles within those businesses, and such roles are important in order to take care of business. Circles are peer structured. Everyone has equal say. Decisions are made by consensus. If any member of a business enters a Heart Circle, it is as a peer rather as an employer or employee. For example, a person playing the role of supervisor must decide if dropping that role while in the Heart Circle serves the business. Sometimes it may and sometimes not. This is a tricky one.

Schools

The inner life of children is completely left behind in most schools today. Every child deserves to have a safe place within the school environment to express what they are feeling and wanting, to talk about their relationships with classmates and teachers, and to learn how to follow their own hearts around what they are inspired to learn.

It is relatively easy to organize Heart Circle in schools if there is political and administrative support for doing so. Heart Circle could also play a significant role on university and college campuses. Circle provides an ideal environment for more mature students to experientially explore heart-activation while staying focused on academics, as well as the art of creating community.

Phone or Internet

While it is ideal to be in the physical presence of one another, Heart Circle can happen through teleconferencing calls or through various Internet platforms. They still work beautifully long distance.

I like to encourage people from different countries and cultures to form one-on-one Heart Circles. Are you old enough to remember pen pals, where children exchanged letters and family photos with someone from a different country? I had a pen pal living in Indonesia when we were both thirteen. I am excited by what's possible today for people of all ages who want to connect with others from different cultures. I'm interested in Circle Pals, where we connect beyond our own national borders and mental framework.

Prisons

We will look back fifty years from now and wonder how we allowed prisons in their current form to ever exist. Until that time, the Heart Circle process can serve people who are serving time. There is heart and humanity in this process. Our prisons can use this.

Organizations

Many people doing service within NGOs and not-for-profit organizations are already heart-centered in their service work. Heart Circle is a good match for these kinds of organizations.

Spiritual Communities

As I mentioned previously, most spiritual organizations are organized around one teacher or a specific set of teachings. These groups sometimes underutilize the synergistic power of individuals connecting with one another within their organizations. Playing the role of spiritual teacher is important, but it can also lead to concretizing that role if the teacher or the students consciously or unconsciously agree to remain in their roles rather than transform beyond them. Heart Circle can help free both the teacher and the students if both are willing to be fully-integrated, equal, sovereign members of their community.

Chapter 13 takes us to two topics that are woven into every Heart Circle: Core-Unworthiness and The Ground of Well-Being. They provide a perfect counter-balance for one another.

CRAZY MENTOR TALK

I asked my crazy mentor
About how to live my life
Translated word for word
She offered me this advice:

"Go way around the road that's straight
Jog past right and sprint past wrong
Sit much longer than your body can stand
Walk across the Arctic snow
Whistling *Way Down South in Dixie.*

Play only games that have no endings
Sing only songs no one remembers
Paint a gorgeous picture that's three-miles long
Catch a falling star as it shoots across your soul.

Ask your cat to tell you everything she knows
Ride the painted stallion who answers only to you
Bring home the dog you've always wanted
Duplicate the pride in the cougar's eye.

Enjoy yourself when you think you are lost
Don't give advice when your best friend cries
Live like musicians whose work is what they play
Tear off the mask that looks exactly like you.

Wash your lover's body with rose oil and cream
Make love in the sea before the dolphins disappear
Digest the broken glass that's swallowed in a quarrel
Dance with your partner across the floor of Time.

End every war before the first shot is fired
Leave behind the prisoners who prefer to stay at home
Speak from the wild place that makes politicians tremble
Bow to the child who was never taught to fear.

Entertain a crowd that's eaten far too much
Build your own house that's mostly made of glass
Swing from a vine that's connected to nothing
Beg a meal from beggars
Then return their bread with gold.

See your world connected to a thread inside your soul
Wonder where you lost your mind, then give it no more thought
Know that love's the answer when the answer can't be found
Know that love's the answer when the answer can't be found."

13

HEART CIRCLE BOOKENDS

To understand Heart Circle, it's necessary to experientially explore the complexities of these next two topics. They are also two of the most important stories intertwining themselves throughout our lives.

Core-Unworthiness

Core-unworthiness is the deep-seated *experiential belief* that we are existentially, now and forevermore, unworthy of being loved. This can also be experienced as never-ending self-criticism, as a willingness to give love but not receive it, or as a profound sense of being disconnected from life. Modern psychology and its offshoots are laying down pathways for understanding it, but that understanding is still in its infancy. Psychology has only existed for a mere hundred years or so.

It's possible that many spiritual teachers and seekers throughout history have bypassed core-unworthiness and focused only on the transcendent spiritual aspects of Oneness (non-duality) or divine devotion (worship). Many of them may not have faced their own self-hatred or internal split. For an extreme image of this, think of penitent people whipping themselves while praying to God. That's a core-unworthiness bypass. Closer to home, think of people who can give love to others but who have great difficulty with self-love or receiving love.

In my own life, I've not experienced anything more difficult than feeling and facing core-unworthiness. First of all, it is usually hidden deep within the subconscious mind. It is much deeper than self-esteem issues, or being self-critical, or not believing we're as good as others. It's a deeper doubt—conditioned, and wired into our nervous systems—that we are acceptable or worthy of love as we are.

Secondly, core-unworthiness comes with utter terror. If it isn't terrifying, it's not core-unworthiness. I personally understand the guy beating himself silly instead of facing his own existential feeling of unworthiness! Physical pain is nothing compared to that. Hand me the branch any day.

The third difficulty in facing core-unworthiness is that it's not a one-time thing. As a conditioned belief system, its roots go deep into both the personal and collective psyche and have many offshoots. It must be re-visited many times, over time.

From my experience, the Christian fixation on Original Sin is a result of the church taking core-unworthiness and, in gambling terms, doubling down on it. They took people's deepest fear—that they are unworthy of love—and used it to bring them into their organizational program. They did this by proclaiming that we are, in fact, born into sin, that we are *unworthy by nature*. The "only way" out of this unworthiness is to accept that Jesus is the only Son of God who sacrificed his life in order to make us worthy. According to church doctrine, if we believe this, our unworthiness is forgiven simply because we believe it. If we don't believe it, we're told we're destined to live in hell forever. How harsh is that?

The obvious irony is that Jesus was delivering the good news that we're *lovable by nature* and that unworthiness is an illusion. He offered his own love to everyone around him as proof that they were lovable. When he asked people to believe *in him,* he was saying simply to *believe him* that they were infinitely lovable. That we are made of love. That God *is* love.

He was saying, in effect, that first loving oneself is the only way of dismantling core-unworthiness and its illusionary belief that we aren't lovable. When we are willing to love ourselves, we either have to let go of the belief that we're unlovable or stay in the temporary hell of thinking that we are unworthy of love. *We leave the hell of disconnection and unworthiness the moment we receive love.*

But there is a catch to this. In order to dismantle the illusion of core-unworthiness, we have to conciously experience the depth of feeling unlovable. We have to admit to ourselves that we actually think and feel that we're unlovable. This is basically *self-confession*, as if to say, "Wow, I actually believe that I am unworthy of love! Isn't that amazing? I've been walking around with this misperception all my life without fully realizing it." We don't confess to *being* unworthy. We confess to mistakenly *thinking* we are unworthy. There is a huge difference between these two confessions. The fundamentalist Christians goofed on this one.

Being willing to fully feel the buried terror of unworthiness is the first stage of coming out of core-unworthiness. The second stage is choosing to let self-love or love from others in, even while feeling fully unloved. This is tricky. For many of us, surrendering to love is not that difficult. But surrendering to love while fully feeling the utter terror that we are unworthy of it is another thing altogether! Yet that is what healing core-unworthiness requires.

This can explain why so many religious and spiritual leaders fall from the lofty ideals they preach. While they may have connected to the higher realms of non-dual awareness or religious devotion, if they haven't fully felt their own hidden core-unworthiness, they will often create some kind of sex, power, or money scandal. When their scandalous actions are made public, and everyone is saying how terrible they are instead of how great they are, they have easier access to their own hidden thoughts of how terrible they are. If they are willing to learn from their fall and witness their own self-loathing, they have a greater chance of coming into deep, humble self-love because they are in the bottom of their fall rather than at the top of their game.

On the level of the absolute, there is no core-unworthiness. It's only conditioned thoughts tied up with shock and deep emotional pain. On the level of the relative, facing core-unworthiness is spectacularly difficult. It is much easier to go into non-dualism, or transcendent love of the Divine, or stay stuck in the business of everyday life.

One of the reasons I love Heart Circle is that it is an intentional social environment in which people can deal with core-unworthiness much more openly and easily than dealing with it alone. When people sitting in circle give us their loving, undivided attention when we ask for it, and when they care about us over time, our core belief about whether or not we're worthy of the love they are giving will eventually surface. This will happen in its own time, without a need for the unworthiness to be eliminated or psychologically processed. Love brings up anything that is unlike itself so that it can be felt and then released in love.

Our willingness to fully feel and face core-unworthiness ends up being our most direct portal into love.

The Ground of Well-Being

Perhaps the greatest opportunity available within a Heart Circle is to experientially explore what can be called the *The Ground of Well-Being*: that everything is okay regardless of any inner or outer circumstance. It is the reality upon which Heart Circle is built. I want to share my perspective about the The Ground of Well-Being, beginning with what I hold that it is *not*.

First, the The Ground of Well-Being is *not* a belief. Believing that everything is okay, that we are love, that we are part of a greater whole, isn't necessary for these things to be true. They're already true, whether we believe them or not. Believing does not make them so. We also don't have to believe that everything is okay because someone else *made* it okay by doing this or that. It isn't true that we are lovable because someone loves us or has saved us. This is superstition. Everything is already okay, regardless of anyone or anything else. Period.

The Ground of Well-Being is *not* an idea. Instead, it is just "what is." A tree is not an idea; it's a tree. My idea of it isn't required. Because the The Ground of Well-Being isn't an idea, it can't be turned into a philosophy or a religion where we have the luxury of adhering to it or not. It's more like gravity; our mind has no say in the matter.

The Ground of Well-Being is *not* a feeling. Everything is okay, not because it feels okay; it's okay whether we feel it or not. If well-being were a feeling, it would only be true when we were feeling it. Knowing that everything is okay does feel good, but feeling good is a by-product of being grounded in this awareness.

Being awake and present is *not* a way to rationalize or explain what is happening to us. For example, it's not like telling ourselves, "It's okay that my sister died because I know life is perfect and therefore there's some perfect reason why she died." This may be a comforting thought, but the comfort remains only as long as we can sustain that thought. Thoughts come and go in a flash. Instead, we have the opportunity to fully feel the loss of someone we love while at the same time maintaining our awareness that there is perfection in whatever is present.

Accessing the The Ground of Well-Being is *not* about dissociation or emotional numbing. *It is about liberating ourselves from thinking, rather than doubling our efforts to think positively.* When we witness and fully feel our painful emotions, they can enliven us rather than squeeze the life out of us.

Experiencing that everything is okay is *not* about blind acceptance of what is. It's not about giving up our true response to what is happening even when we see the perfection in it. We don't have to surrender our outrage around a social injustice nor our desire to right something clearly wrong. A rapist may be part of the divine order of things, but so is my righteous sword drawn to prevent the rape.

More than anything else, being awake and present does *not* require affirmations. Most affirmations simply rearrange our thoughts without taking us beyond thought and into stillness. Telling ourselves that life is perfect, or taping this message to our mirrors, keeps us focused in our mind. While the words of the affirmation may be true, they still end up being mental propaganda, an effort to convince ourselves of what's true rather than feeling what's true.

These are a few things that The Ground of Being is *not*. So, what *is* it?

Heart Circle provides a social environment that supports each member in finding out. A Heart Circle is a Heart Circle, in part, because its very nature and ultimate purpose are to support people in coming into their own realization of the The Ground of Well-Being, in their own way and within their own time.

Because the Ground of Well-Being is not a belief, there is no pressure to convince people that it's true. There is simply ongoing social support to explore whether or not it's true. As the architect of the Heart Circle process, I have woven into its design my own conclusion about the The Ground of Well-Being. No one needs to agree with me in order to be in Heart Circle. That is part of the beauty: people in Circle can believe whatever they want. At the same time, The Ground of Well-Being is still foundational to Heart Circle.

As we head towards book closure, we come to the last basic question: "How do we start a Heart Circle?" Chapter 14 gives a step by step answer.

GOD IS QUITE AN ARTIST

God is quite an artist
He sculpted you and me
Molded all the mountains
Water-colored all the seas.

He painted all the deserts
Pastelled green the grass and trees
God is quite an Artist
He sculpted you and me.

She works in rock and bronze and wood
But also flesh and bone
She paints with artist's mastery
Everything that's known.

He shades the newborn baby's skin
With hereditary tone
Fashions stars and galaxies
Giving night a daylight loan.

She weaves a sunset tapestry
For all the world to see
The planet is Her gallery
All creatures enter free.

He charcoals black the sky at night
And repaints the world at dawn.
He writes a million plays at once
Each play a lifetime long.

God is quite an Artist
She sculpted you and me.

14

HOW TO CREATE
AND SUSTAIN
A HEART CIRCLE

Step One: Find a Heart Circle Partner

To start a Heart Circle, begin by finding *one* other person to be in a Heart Circle with you. As I've already suggested, don't start with a larger group of people. Whether it is within your circle of friends, your family, business, school, or organization, ensure that your Heart Circle partner is someone you like and respect. While you don't have to be best friends, you must share a certain resonance and a common willingness to explore the Heart Circle process together. Although it's best that you live in the same area and can meet face-to-face, Heart Circles can also occur online or on the phone and still be quite powerful.

Step Two: Read This Book

Make sure both of you have read this book. Many people have been in other kinds of circles and may think they are the same as a Heart Circle. Even with all the similarities to traditional wisdom circles, Heart Circles have a very specific purpose, format, and set of agreements. The purpose of this section of the book is to clarify what a Heart Circle is and how it functions.

Step Three: Agree with Heart Circle Purpose

Before meeting formally in a Circle, get together informally to discuss and agree upon the purpose and procedures of Heart Circle. The purpose of Heart Circle is to support one another in Heart-Awakening: becoming more Clear, Present, Real, Connected, and Heart-Directed in life.

Step Four: Agree with These Heart Circle Procedural Guidelines

During your initial informal meeting, discuss and agree on the following essential Heart Circle guidelines:

- Confidentiality
- No Third-Party Talk
- Taking Responsibility
- Resolving Conflicts Directly and Quickly
- No Drugs or Alcohol
- Notification
- Commitment
- Consensus
- No Confrontation
- Spontaneous Participation
- Clear Time Boundaries
- No Fixing One Another
- Enjoyment
- Additional Agreements

Confidentiality

Because a Heart Circle is a place where members are free to speak intimately about what is happening in their personal lives, it is essential to have agreements around confidentiality. The general rule is this: "What happens in Circle stays in Circle." If there is any gray area around what is confidential and what is not, always check back with the group members for clarification before sharing with someone outside the group.

Within each Circle, members must grapple with their definition of confidentiality and then create their own agreements around keeping it. Once these agreements are in place, they must be honored. It is suggested that if confidentiality is broken, this lapse needs to be brought up in Circle so the person who broke it is clear about how vital confidentiality is to the integrity of the Circle. A two-strike warning is given. If it is broken a second time, it may be a good idea to ask the person breaking confidentiality to leave the Circle. Confidentiality is that important. Breaking confidentiality will always break the Circle, regardless of whether the Circle is made up of two people or ten. In order for members to feel safe to share anything important to them, they must know that what they share will not be shared with others outside of Circle.

No Third-Party Talk

During Heart Circle, talking analytically or negatively about other people who aren't present in Circle will significantly lower the overall vitality and integrity of the group. If you have an issue with someone, your commitment is to speak to that person directly, rather than with others inside or outside your Circle. This agreement replaces third-party talk with direct, honest communication.

Taking Responsibility

When speaking in the Circle, taking responsibility for your own experience will help keep your Circle vital. This means speaking for yourself and not for others, using "I" statements rather than "we" or "you" statements.

Resolve Conflicts Directly and Quickly

Resolve conflicts that may arise within your Circle as soon as they arise, rather than letting them fester and crystallize. You agree that you want to be open, direct, and clear about what you're feeling and wanting, while listening compassionately to what the other Heart Circle members are feeling and wanting.

No Drugs or Alcohol

As with driving a car, mixing drugs, alcohol, or smoking with Circle doesn't work. Exploring how we can consciously transform our emotional and energetic state is impossible if we have already used drugs or alcohol to do so.

Notification

If we can't be at a particular Heart Circle meeting, or if we're going to be late, it's important to notify at least one other member beforehand.

Commitment

It's best to decide together on how long members want to initially explore being in Circle together. Four-week commitments usually work well, though some may choose to begin with eight. During this time, making Heart Circle meetings a high priority is essential for the Circle to be effective. At the end of the initial four or eight weeks, you can decide if you want to continue, and for how long. You can also decide then whether you want to add new members. In terms of commitment to your Circle, there will obviously be times that something keeps you from attending, like a child's school play or being out of town. This agreement is not saying that you will be at every meeting, but that you truly want to be at every meeting. It's saying that Circle is a priority.

Consensus

There may be times in the life of a Heart Circle when decisions will have to be made, such as bringing new people into the group, adjusting meeting times, and other changes. These decisions must be made through consensus. *Everyone* must agree. Once a person is a member of a Heart Circle, it is their Circle. Everyone has full say in what happens in Circle, or else that ownership is meaningless. If there isn't consensus around an issue, the agreement is to keep working on it until there is.

No Confrontation

Heart Circles are *not* about confronting each other or holding each other accountable. Those kinds of groups exist elsewhere. In Heart Circle, any member can ask the others for support with something but, in general, members are accountable only to themselves. A member *can* ask to be held accountable in whatever specific way that person wants. For example, if someone wants help breaking an addictive pattern, they can ask others for the kind of help that a Twelve-Step sponsor might provide. At the same time, this specific component about confrontation and accountability holds that Heart Circle isn't designed for either confrontation or accountability.

Clear Time Boundaries

Beginning and ending Heart Circle at clear, designated times is important. This is more important than it may seem. Trust and safety are established when each Circle member knows and honors their agreed-upon beginning and ending times. If everyone wants to extend the meeting as closure time approaches, taking a moment to agree on a new ending time is important. Circles with lax beginning and ending times are far less powerful than those Circles with clear time boundaries.

Spontaneous Participation

Most of us were trained in school to raise our hands if we wanted to speak, and to not interrupt others when they are speaking. Proponents of this kind of linear order often use moral judgments and punishment to enforce it, proclaiming that it is "rude" to interrupt and there will be painful consequences if you do. The rationale is that there would be chaos if everyone spoke whenever they wanted.

Yet, if we look at the way friends communicate, there's no linear order. They don't raise their hands and say, "Excuse me, Linda. May I speak now?" Friends replace linear speaking order with an internally guided process that automatically calibrates when it's time to speak and when it's time to listen. This freedom helps develop a kind of social intelligence that gives everyone an opportunity to speak whenever they want, while being sensitive to everyone else's desire to do the same. Heart Circle relies on this internal calibration to maximize people's spontaneity so that the Circle stays alive and creative. Heart Circle members can talk anytime they want to talk, while practicing being sensitive to others.

No talking stick or speaking order is required in Heart Circle! Sharing talk time is better guided by our innate sensitivity to one another than by passing a stick or raising hands.

No Fixing One Another

This agreement is essential for a Heart Circle, or any relationship, to function effectively. If someone shares their deep feelings or concerns about any issue in their lives, they must know that other people within the Circle will not try to fix them, offer solutions, or give unsolicited advice. In general, we all want to be heard and seen, rather than advised and corrected. Being witnessed in this way makes it easier for us to find our own internal direction, without the interference of well-meaning advice givers. With this said, anyone can ask for feedback or advice from other Circle members whenever they want.

Enjoyment

There is a simple *intent-agreement* that you each want to enjoy the time you spend together.

Additional Agreements

In addition to the *required* agreements named above, Heart Circle members can create other agreements, as long as they are consensual.

Step Five: Agree to Use the Heart Circle Format

Still within your informal meeting, before officially starting a Circle, members agree on the Heart Circle format. This format, or agenda, is meant to be a flowing guideline, rather than a formalized procedure set in stone. We don't need a timer or a conversation cop to regulate what happens in Circle, but we do need a focused sensitivity to stay within the parameters outlined here. As you follow this format, you can make adjustments based upon your own experience of what works and doesn't work. You will find your group rhythms and preferences. As previously noted, the components of a Heart Circle meeting follow a specific order:

- Make Agreements to Be Clear
- Tune in to Be Present
- Check in to Be Real
- Give/Receive Appreciative Feedback to Be Connected
- Hold Space for One Another to Be Heart-Directed
- Close

Make Agreements to Be Clear

Once you have made initial agreements about the purpose and function of Heart Circle, you don't have to keep revisiting those agreements each time you meet. You can always negotiate new agreements or review the older agreements when the desire or need to do so arises. This keeps your Circle flexible and healthy. For example, you may initially agree on a starting and ending time, and then find that you need more time or less. New agreements can be made as long as there is consensus with the change. The basic procedural agreements listed above *cannot* be changed, however, for your Circle to remain a Heart Circle. For example, you may decide as a Circle that you want to allow drug use during your circle time. This is up to you as a circle. It just won't be a Heart Circle if you decide to do so.

Tune in to Be Present

The actual Heart Circle begins with sitting together in silence for several minutes. There are no "shoulds" in this process. Eyes can be open or shut. Hands can be held or not. The allotted time for tuning in can be whatever the group wants it to be. I personally like holding hands, so that when people are complete with tuning in, they just let go of the hands. If members want some kind of tune-in ritual other than silence, it must be agreed upon by consensus. For example, in a family Heart Circle, the parents can't simply decide that the way the group will tune in is with a prayer; this happens only if all the family members agree.

Check in to Be Real

Each person takes a few minutes to check in. A check-in covers one or both of these questions: What are you feeling right now? And briefly, what has happened since the last meeting that is significant to you?

The check-in is best kept short. Having short check-ins also gives members the opportunity to be concise and direct in communicating what they're feeling, without having to go into their story around their feelings or experience. This is a wonderful skill to have in communicating with others inside or outside of Circle. If someone isn't sure what they are feeling or what they want to say, they can use those few minutes to self-inquire, in stillness, to find out.

The check-in helps each person come into the present moment. You're notifying each other what you're bringing into the Circle as the meeting begins. For example, one member may come into the Circle and say, "I am feeling anxious. My father ended up in the hospital yesterday and needs surgery." This information allows the others to know immediately what that member is experiencing. The meeting will organically arrange itself to accommodate him or her as the meeting progresses. If this isn't shared at the start of the meeting, others may sense something is going on with another member, but not actually know what it is.

Checking in is always optional. You can pass if you don't want to share what you're feeling. In Circle, there is no pressure to do anything unless you want to do it. It is a be-as-you-are party.

Give/Receive Appreciative Feedback to Be Connected

This part of the Heart Circle format provides time for anyone in the Circle to say something that they appreciate about any other person in the Circle. Only one person at a time talks to whomever is receiving the appreciation. The receiving person may respond back to the one giving the feedback, like a private conversation between two people, while the rest of the Circle members listen in.

What keeps this appreciative feedback from being contrived is that it comes with one specific suggestion: whatever you are going to say to another person is best if it comes up spontaneously in the moment, as you look around the Circle. This kind of intuitive response has invariably more sincerity and heart woven into it than when we try to think of something appreciative to say to another person. It has nothing to do with giving someone a compliment to make them feel better, or to indirectly raise their appreciation of you. It's something that pops into your awareness, and sharing it can be as surprising to you as to the person being appreciated.

There's a second possibility, other than giving appreciative feedback. We can ask each other "questions from the heart." Using the same spontaneous pop-up style, we can ask another member of the Circle anything we sincerely want to know about them, as long we are reasonably certain that the question will draw positive memory or information from the person being asked. For example, we wouldn't ask them about the most difficult thing they had to face while growing up. We'd ask what was one of the happiest experiences they had while growing up.

This is not as sappy as it may initially sound. In fact, it can have an astounding effect on the connections between Circle members. When people are given authentic appreciative feedback, or are asked something that the asker is genuinely interested in hearing, a heart connection is almost invariably created between the two people. Even though the process is formatted, it becomes a heart-opening experience, not only for the two having the exchange, but also for the rest of the Circle members. It creates a sense of well-being in the Circle.

These two-person exchanges are kept short—two or three minutes. It's important to note that people have complete freedom to *not* give feedback if nothing comes to mind. This is something that must be experienced first-hand in order to comprehend the depth of connection that is possible in this part of the Heart Circle format.

Hold Space for One Another to Be Heart-Directed

The major portion of Heart Circle time is for members to gain greater clarity about anything they truly want. Another way of saying this is that each person is given time to focus on what they want in order to become more Clear, Present, Real, Connected, and Heart-Directed, given their current life situation. This pretty well covers any topic imaginable. The Five Ways of Being act as an infinite umbrella of topic possibility.

The act of identifying and feeling what we truly want has several advantages:

- Identifying what we truly want is often inspiring. It gives us access to a greater sense of wellbeing. It's enjoyable. And it adds dimension and depth to our self-connection when we connect to our soul-wants.

- Knowing and feeling what we want sets in motion the Law of Attraction. What we focus on, we draw to us. By deliberately focusing on what we want, we deliberately draw to ourselves the same.

- If we don't know what we want, the obvious way to find out is to ask ourselves. When we are willing to sit in the unknown of this question with quiet, easy focus, an answer will often come to us "out of the blue." Identifying what we want on a moment-to-moment basis gives us internal heart-direction in life. Being internally guided by our hearts replaces living on automatic pilot—going through the motions of life, without internal inspiration behind what we are doing.

Knowing what we want will often bring up our fears, self-doubts, and conditioning around receiving whatever that may be. Dealing with these fears and conditioning is a large part of what Heart Awakening actually is.

When we understand these basic functions of identifying what we truly want, we tend to live more intentionally. In order to receive in life more of what we do want, rather than more of what we don't want, we must get clearer about what we actually want. Heart Circles are essentially about making our wants, preferences, and heartfelt desires more deliberate and conscious. As we do, we manifest more of what truly enlivens and delights us in life.

If there are four or more people in a Heart Circle, it is best to informally allocate time for members to explore what they want. However, never use a timer for this. By allocating time, I simply mean that there is a general agreement for each person to take five to fifteen minutes, depending on the size of the Circle. There may also be a Circle meeting in which one person takes all of the Circle time, because whatever has come up really needs that kind of time and attention, and everyone in the Circle senses and agrees with this need.

It's essential for everyone in the Circle to have the freedom to agree or disagree to hold space for any person asking for it. Just because someone wants attention doesn't automatically mean we are obliged to give it. The agreement is always in play for each Circle member to be real—to give their true response in any given moment, rather than acting out of obligation or politeness. Because everyone in the Circle has agreed to give honest responses, there is greater freedom to say "no," so the person asking for attention knows that people really want to give their attention when they say "yes." If someone doesn't want to give his or her attention to another, everyone in the Circle can work out what happens next until there is consensus. Maybe the person not wanting to give attention needs the group's attention first. Again, this is what good friends spontaneously do outside of Heart Circle:

"Hey, Mark. I want to tell you about what happened last night."

"Jack, I'm really interested, but can I first tell you what's happening for me right now?"

"Sure! What's up?"

An important aspect of Heart Circles is that they continue over time. The same members meet together week after week, and sometimes year after year. Because deliberately creating what we want—in ourselves and in our lives—is an ongoing process, we need social structures that are also ongoing. These structures allow us to explore together how each person is progressing with the creative process. For example, if one member wants to find work that is more fulfilling than their current employment, it may take weeks, months, or even years to manifest. Having a group of friends who are deliberately supporting this person over time can be invaluable. It is what friendships are for—mutually following and supporting each other's journey towards greater and greater life fulfillment.

Close

Creating closure means taking a few minutes at the end of the Circle meeting to be still, in order to feel whatever impact being in Circle may have had. It's also a time to feel the field of connection that is often generated between members during a Heart Circle. As a result of practicing being Clear, Present, Real, Connected, and Heart-Directed with one another, there will usually be a strong, often palpable, resonant field or quality created within the Circle. Sitting in this shared field is nurturing, enlivening, and deeply relaxing.

Closure can also be a time for each member to say a few words about what he or she needs in order to feel complete with the time spent in that Circle.

Closure is never a time for opening up new topics.

There is a bit of magical wonder involved with closing a Circle in this way. Each Circle meeting has an energetic life of its own, as do all relationships and social gatherings. When it's time for that form to end and something new to begin, consciously ending it, rather than just letting it end without closure, allows for a smooth energetic transition from one form to the next.

To close your Heart Circle meeting, like when tuning in, sit together in silence with hands held or not, eyes open or closed, for a minute or two. Each person then takes a few seconds to say whether they feel complete or incomplete for that Circle meeting. Another option is for members to say one or two words describing how they are feeling as they close: "I'm feeling really inspired!" or "I'm feeling frustrated that I didn't take as much time as I wanted to tonight. I am incomplete." Acknowledging that we are incomplete somehow makes us complete. In another example, someone could say, "I feel grateful for Circle tonight. I am complete."

Step Six: Agree to a Time and Place to Meet

After coming into agreement about the purpose of Heart Circle and the procedural guidelines, choose a time to meet weekly, preferably for at least four weeks. Meeting bi-monthly instead of weekly can work, but if you miss one week, you won't meet for a month, and this can break the continuity of your Circle.

The quality of the environment where you choose to hold your Heart Circle will affect the quality of your Circle experience. The best places to meet are cozy homes, with no outside interruptions, and where there is comfortable seating. Meeting in restaurants or in public places doesn't provide enough privacy or focus for a Heart Circle. It's best to not eat while meeting. It decreases your ability to focus on what you are feeling, thinking, and wanting.

Ensure that no one can overhear what is happening as you meet, and that people don't walk into your meeting space once the Circle begins. This is especially important if you're meeting in each other's homes where other household members live.

Sit in comfortable chairs, sofas, or on floor cushions. Sitting around empty space encourages intimacy and connection. Sitting around a table encourages taking action.

Step Seven: Meet for an Initial Four or Eight Weeks

Together, find your own way with this format and with these procedural guidelines. Trust. Experiment. Enjoy.

Step Eight: Decide What's Next

At the end of the initial four or eight weeks of Circle, decide if you want to continue your Circle together. If you have consensus desire to continue, consider expanding it by inviting one or two more people into it. You could invite other family members if you are a family Heart Circle, other friends if it's a friends Heart Circle, etc. With these new people, repeat the same Eight Steps the initial two of you went through.

Heart Circle can form within any group, using the mini Heart Circle pairing approach. For example, if six members within a family want to be in Heart Circle together, they can begin by pairing into three mini Heart Circles. After the initial pairing time is complete, all six may want to start meeting together in one family Circle.

•   •   •

How a Heart Circle Is Facilitated

- All Member Facilitation
- Time Allotment
- Keeping Focus on Heart-Direction
- Giving and Receiving Attention
- Holding Space
- Dealing with Emotional Pain
- Being Guided by Intuition
- The Top Three Circle Topics

All Member Facilitation

The entire essence of Heart Circle facilitation, whether with two people or ten, is that each person is responsible for whatever happens in their Circle. Thus the Circle becomes what everyone wants it to become. All-member facilitation is possible when the following agreements are in place and being practiced:

- Each person in Circle is *equally* responsible for the facilitation of the Circle. This doesn't mean each person takes a turn facilitating, but rather that all members are continuously facilitating the meeting collectively at the same time.

- Each person self-facilitates Circle through his or her willingness to be authentic in responding to whatever is happening in the Circle. If one person doesn't like something that is happening, they agree to state this and then say what they want to be happening that isn't happening. If people want two different things, they negotiate until consensus is reached.

- Each person is equally responsible for making sure that the basic Heart Circle agreements are kept during each Circle meeting;

i.e., meet and close on time, no third-party talk, keeping the focus on feelings and wants, etc.

Time Allotment

The basic Heart Circle agenda provides a time structure that is relatively easy to follow. The tune-in takes two to five minutes. Each person then takes a few minutes to check in. Appreciative feedback usually is complete in five to fifteen minutes, depending on the size of the group. The bulk of the time in Circle is allotted for members taking time, one by one, to focus on what they want or need in order to be more clear, present, real, connected and heart-directed in their lives. Closure then takes a total of two to five minutes. In general, Heart Circles are designed to last from thirty to sixty minutes when two people meet, and ninety to one hundred twenty minutes for a larger group.

Within this time structure, members decide who speaks according to who wants to speak next. If two people want to speak at the same time, they work that out between themselves. If someone doesn't want to speak, there is never pressure to do so.

As mentioned before, there is no need to formally time each other using timers and rigid thinking. This process is much more relaxed than that. It is a good idea, however, to have a clock visible in the room so that everyone can be aware of time as the Circle proceeds. Therefore, if there are six people in the Circle and the check-in is taking more than twenty minutes of the two-hour meeting, someone may want to move the check-in along.

With this said, it is possible that, on occasion, the suggested time allotment is altered because everyone wants it altered. For example, the tune-in may be so enjoyable that people want it to continue for an extra few minutes.

Keeping the Focus on Heart-Direction

Because the heart of the Heart Circle format is in holding space for members to find out what they are truly wanting, knowing how to keep this time focused on what each member wants is essential for a Heart Circle to be effective. In order to better answer the ongoing, moment-to-moment question, "What do you want?" we can get more specific with these questions:

- What do you want in this moment? Given both what you are feeling right now and what is happening in your life at this time, what do you really want? What would feel good to you? What answer pops up within you when you ask this question? Also, if you are feeling bad, what do you want in order to feel better?

- What do you want in a particular time frame? What do you want in the next hour, tonight, tomorrow, over the weekend, this summer, in the coming year, in the next ten years?

- What do you want relative to a specific issue in your life? For example, if a socially challenged co-worker frustrates you, what do you want in relationship to this person? If you have a health issue, what do you want in order to be healthier?

- What do you want relative to a specific event coming up in your life? If you are going to a family gathering, what do you want while you are there? Or for a camping trip? Or a meeting?

- What do you want relative to being internally "guided?" What does your heart want? What would most benefit the greater good? What wants to occur right now?

- What do you want relative to a specific area of your life?

  Your partnership or marriage: If you're not in partnership, do you want to be? If you have a partner, do you want more intimacy, more fun, better communication? What do you truly want? It can be anything.

Your family: If you have children, do you want to spend more time with them? If you have a brother, do you want to call him this week? What do you want in relationship to your favorite cousin?

Your friendships: What do you want in relationship to any of your friends? Do you want more friends? Fewer friends? More presence with them?

Your community: What do you want in relationship to your community? You can define this term however you choose, and it can include political or civic involvement. It can also include your neighborhood or the people you work with. It generally refers to those people who have an active interest in your well-being and you in theirs.

Your work: Do you love your work? If you don't, what do you want to do relative to that? If you do, what do you want in order to love it even more?

Your money: How do you want to manage your income or your lack of income? How do you want to relate to money?

Your play/leisure: Do you want more leisure time? What do you want to do that's fun? This topic includes vacations, sports, connection with nature, hobbies, and anything else you love to do for pleasure and joy.

Your health: Do you want to take better care of yourself? This includes your physical, emotional, mental, energetic, and spiritual health. They are all listed under "health," because each area affects and overlaps the other—that is, your mental health affects your physical health and your spiritual health affects your emotional health.

Your learning/creativity: What do you want to learn next? How do you want to express yourself creatively?

The details of your life: When do you want to do the laundry next? Do you want to go shopping for clothes? Do you want to water your plants today?

When you identify what you want, instead of looking at what you *have to do* in order to manifest that want, look at what you *want relative to* your desire. By continuing to stay with what you want, there is a better chance of enjoying the process of attracting it to you. This will require that you take action to receive what you desire, but *those actions will be in harmony with your heart.*

Heart Circle provides an environment for us to better know what we're feeling and desiring in life. Ultimately, the question is, "What do I want in order to be more Clear, Present, Real, Connected, and Heart-Directed? What do I want in order to Heart Awaken?"

Giving and Receiving Attention

One of my favorite all-time quotes is from the Dalai Lama:

Wisdom arises through the simple act of giving someone or something your full attention. Attention is primordial intelligence, consciousness itself. It joins the perceiver and the perceived in a unifying field of awareness. It is the healer of separation.

The quality of all human interaction is largely based on the quality of the attention we give each other in that interaction. *Love is attention.* More than anything else, Heart Circle is a place to deliberately give and receive attention, i.e. love. The following process can be spoken out loud or simply implied:

One person can ask, "May I have your attention for a few minutes while I find out what I am feeling and wanting about_____?" The Circle members answer either yes or no. If all answer yes, members get still and present in relationship to the one who asked. Asking directly and out loud, "May I have your attention for a few minutes?" can be surprisingly powerful. With this direct request, it's often possible to literally *feel* the attention given. Asking for attention so directly can also give us an opportunity to see if thoughts or feelings come up around being unworthy to receive it. However, when attention is asked for and given, it is just as the Dalai Lama says: "It is the healer of separation."

Sometimes, Heart Circle members can ask for attention without using it to inquire into anything specific. They may just want to receive and feel the attention (love) being offered by the other Circle members for a few minutes. When we are open to receiving attention in this manner, it can often feel like *bathing* in love.

If everyone agrees to hold space for another, it is good to get a general idea of how long that person wants attention. Holding our attention in short spurts of time is much easier than long periods of time: "May I have your attention for the next five or so minutes while I look at what I want in relationship to my business meeting next Tuesday?"

Holding Space

Holding Space is giving your full attention to another person by quieting your mind and coming into your heart so that your compassionate presence can amplify and support the other person's inquiry into what they're feeling and wanting about any topic or issue for which they want inner guidance or relief from suffering or the experience of being felt or being seen by you.

Let's try it again with more space, since it's about "holding space".

Holding Space is giving your full attention

to another person

by quieting your mind

and coming into your heart

so that your compassionate presence

can amplify and support

the other person's inquiry

into what they're feeling and wanting

about any topic or issue

for which they want inner guidance

or relief from suffering

or the experience of being felt

or being seen

by you.

What are we doing when we give deliberate attention to another? We are actually not *doing* anything. We are definitely *not* "sending energy" to another. We are *not* trying to blank our minds and not think of anything while being attentive to someone. Neither of those two things is required. We simply get still. We tune in to the other, but paradoxically this is often more effective as we tune into ourselves. We feel our own bodies from within, while feeling the energetic field of the group. We listen and witness.

We are free to find our way with this entire process of holding space. There is plenty of room for experimentation. If someone tries to fix or advise another person in Circle, instead of treating this as some sort of terrible agreement violation, it can be used as a learning opportunity to explore the difference between fixing and holding space.

I have caught myself many times trying to fix another person in Circle. Heart Circle is for learning, not for trying to get things right.

Dealing with Emotional Pain

Heart Circles are not designed to be psychological "processing groups" in which members gather together with the purpose to find, feel, and heal their emotional wounds. There are other, clinical settings more appropriate and effective in that endeavor than a Heart Circle. This does not mean, however, that people won't get in touch with deep emotional pain while in the Circle, nor that it's inappropriate for someone to bring his or her pain to the Circle. Whatever comes up in Circle is welcome in Circle.

What do we do when someone in Circle is in deep emotional pain? We *do* nothing. We don't try to fix them. We don't try to get them to go deeper into it nor do we become responsible for their releasing it or working through it. Instead, it's usually more effective to just empathize with them. Empathizing with them can elicit compassion, and with compassion we have better access to our own clear response to them. Empathetically feeling them ironically gives us better boundaries with them: we have greater access to the sense that everything is okay no matter what pain they are experiencing. We don't take on their pain. We're then in a more neutral position to hold space for them, to love them, while they experience their pain.

The response to emotional pain does not end in feeling another's pain and doing nothing. It begins here. The idea is to encourage the person to feel their own pain fully so that, once felt, they then can shift into the question of what they want or need in relationship to their pain. This inquiry itself— "What do you want now that you're feeling what you are feeling?"—will often give someone access to his or her inner guidance, and help them come to a place of peace with the pain.

Being Guided by Intuition

Everyone is intuitive. Some people have learned to identify and trust their intuition more than others. Heart Circle is a place to practice identifying intuitive flashes. The word "practice" is important because intuitive thoughts are subtle and quick. They often come in flashes then disappear, and therefore we can always use help noticing and trusting them. In Heart Circle, we can intentionally create more subtle environments, where the whisper of intuition can be more easily heard. In such environments, not only are we able to hear our intuitive impulses better, but we also receive validation when we share them in Circle.

Top Three Circle Topics

Sitting in thousands of Circles over the last thirty years, I've had an opportunity to witness what issues and topics come up most often. None of these will surprise you. Can you guess the first one?

- Relationships: How do we attract a partner if we don't have one? How do we stay with our partner if we do have one? How do we leave our partner if the relationship isn't healthy? And, much more to the point, why do relationships seem so complicated and difficult? Added to these four topics is a multitude of subtopics like sexuality, male - female differences, and changing gender roles.

- Money and Work: Money problems come up often. This includes debt—not being able to meet expenses or afford something important. Work concerns go right along with it. Having meaningful work, issues of unemployment, conflicts with workers or bosses, and over-working are some of the most common issues that come up in Circle. And then there is our common longing to be in a creative, supportive, well-paying and rewarding work environment.

- Health: Health issues come and go similarly to money problems. However, health issues can affect every aspect of our lives, obviously including whether we live or die. In recent years, health issues have become increasingly tied to money issues because of high health insurance premiums or loss of work income. Health is a major concern to most of us, either with our own health or with the health of those we love.

In Heart Circle, we don't just sit around and discuss these issues. No one says, "Let's all take the next thirty minutes to talk about money." It's not like that. These issues come up when people engage in honest self-reflection and have the freedom and encouragement to explore any aspect of their lives that seems necessary, relevant, or urgent to them in that moment. These topics come up because members are willing to feel into their relationship with these issues as they surface.

Ways Heart Circles Can Weaken

There are predictable ways in which Heart Circles can falter. Knowing what they are is the first defense in preventing them from weakening your Circle.

- Talk Circle
- Problem Solving Circle
- Ignoring Circle Procedural Agreements
- Circle Rigidity
- Wrong Member Fit
- Switching Purpose
- Changing the Heart Circle Format
- Forgetting What's Most Important

Talk Circle

All Heart Circles will have to be vigilant about keeping the focus on what members are feeling and wanting, rather than on what members are thinking, or on their stories. There is a tendency in our culture to use words as a way of staying away from what we are feeling and wanting. We tell long stories when a word or two will do. We have debates over political issues, rather than sharing feelings that come up as a result of these issues. If a Heart Circle turns into talk circle, it will lose its vitality and effectiveness.

Problem-Solving Circle

There will also invariably be a natural tendency for members to come to Circle and share what is wrong with their lives. They will present their life issues as problems, rather than as situations. While there is nothing wrong with this, it will eventually turn the Circle into a place of continual problem sharing. In small doses, this is fine. When it becomes standard procedure week after week, the Heart Circle stops being enjoyable and members lose their enthusiasm for continuing.

There is a good reason why members relate to their issues as problems. We tend to live problematically because we have not been encouraged or trained to look at what we feel and want in relationship to our issues. It's therefore easy to stay stuck in them. We become victims to our life situations because we don't know what we want in relationship to them. Encouraging each other to ask for attention about what we want to create in our lives helps keep us out of perpetual problem mode. Holding space for members to explore what they want in relationship to their life issues, rather than just articulating the issues, enlivens both the one inquiring and the Circle as a whole.

Ignoring Circle Agreements

Keeping Heart Circle agreements is the ultimate way for Heart Circles to stay enjoyable and effective. Breaking these agreements without making new agreements to replace them is the ultimate way of puncturing a Circle's life force.

Every agreement is important. For example, if a member commits to being in circle and then fails to show up week after week, the Circle loses some of its potency. If confidentiality is broken, a Circle can be shattered and not survive. If members don't start and end on time, the

Circle will "leak energy" and not be the safe container it is designed to be.

Any member, at any time, can revisit any of the agreements for renegotiation. For example, if there is an agreement to meet every Monday night for two hours and someone wants to meet on Tuesday for ninety minutes, the meeting time and place can be renegotiated. If someone wants to leave the Circle before the agreed upon interval, there needs to be closure with that person, so that everyone has an opportunity to respond to their leaving.

Circle Rigidity

Some people may have a tendency to interpret the Heart Circle process too literally, to the point that all humor and lightness get squeezed out of it. The Circle process is powerful and has tremendous value. But a Heart Circle must remain adaptive, flexible, and capable of change. This is much more about the *art* of Circle than the *science* of Circle.

For example, it's important that Heart Circle members not get caught in their stories—not talk on and on about what has happened to them. However, there may be situations where talking on and on about something is exactly what a member needs. To tell that person to "get out of their story," without feeling that person's need to tell it, will not be helpful or heart-full.

Another way to concretize, and harm, a Heart Circle is to use it to spiritually judge others. For example, telling someone he or she is "just in their head," or that they need to come down into their heart, is neither necessary nor kind.

Wrong Member Fit

Sometimes a member ends up in the wrong Heart Circle. It's like a mismatched marriage. Sometimes it's simply a misfit. This can cause considerable disturbance to a Circle when one member seems continuously out of sync with what is happening in the rest of the Circle. In this situation, my suggestion is to tread lightly. Find a way to bring up what each person is feeling about this situation, including the response of the person who doesn't seem to fit in.

Three resolutions are possible. First, talking about this issue can bring an opening of heart, and a connective re-synchronization for everyone. The person stays. Second, talking about it makes the person in question realize that they are not a comfortable fit for that Circle, and the person leaves. Or, third, people give feedback to that person that his or her presence is not working for them and they then hold space for that person to have their own feelings and wants around that feedback. What happens from this point is whatever happens. Everyone stays in the process for as long as it takes, until there is resolution by consensus.

In all three situations, the Heart Circle agreement that must always remain in place is that members can *never* tell another Heart Circle member to leave the Circle. The only exception is if that member has broken certain essential agreements, like confidentiality. Circle works by consensus, always. Otherwise, members will not be able to fully feel that it is their Circle. And a Heart Circle always belongs to the members who make it up.

Switching Purpose

The primary purpose of Heart Circle is to support one another in taking the evolutionary leap into Heart Awakening. It's quite easy to lose sight of this purpose and replace it with other purposes. In my experience, there are two other purposes that often replace Heart Awakening. The first is when the primary intent shifts to processing problems and trauma. It's easy to slip into this.

The second replacement purpose is when the primary focus turns to the interrelationships between the people in Circle. The Circle simply forgets about individual awakening, and lets the focus be on building community or strengthening the connection between members. From my experience, community formation is a product of individual Heart Awakening: we come into true community automatically when our hearts open. If this is the other way around, it can lead to people creating a strong social group, but that group will lose touch with the ultimate purpose of personal transformation.

Changing the Heart Circle Format

This is a big one. The Heart Circle format is designed to bring each of the Five Ways of Being into a living, social practice. Just as all five of these Ways of Being work synergistically within each of us, the five elements of Heart Circle process—making agreements, tuning in, checking in, connecting up, and holding space for heart-direction—also work synergistically. One without the other four doesn't work that well.

For example, in the Heart Circle process, members may have a tendency to spend most of their Circle time with long, storied check-ins, leaving little time for holding space around what people want. Or members may skip appreciative feedback because one or more members bring up an issue that seems too urgent to take time for this feedback segment. But each of these specific segments of Circle has a specific function for creating a strong container. For example, giving appreciative feedback *before* focusing on urgent life issues can help establish the sense that everything is okay, no matter what is happening. This sense can give us a greater ability to hold space when those urgent issues are present. As another example, asking for attention while we inquire into what we truly want requires courage and the willingness to be in the Unknown. It's much easier to listen to one another check in. Without fulfilling its primary role of providing space for members to find greater heart-direction, the Circle will lose much of its transformational power.

Heart Circles are designed to create balance in all five of these Ways of Being. Staying within the specified format helps integrate these Ways of Being. For me, this is essential. At the same time, it's nothing to get fanatical about. Every Circle has to find its own way with this.

Forgetting What's Most Important

What keeps a Circle strong, more than anything else, is remembering one essential reason why we are in Heart Circle: to *enjoy* being in the supportive company of those who share the longing to awaken. Enjoying being together with this common intent provides the greatest insurance that the Circle will thrive.

I'm not presenting any of these standard Circle issues as problems. We are all new at building social containers consciously. There is plenty of room for trial and error.

This covers the technical talk about starting your own Heart Circle. Now, as Leonard Cohen musically proclaimed, "It's Closing Time."

You Will Know

How will you know
That your heart has awakened?

Well…
Your crown will open
Your voice will grow mighty
Your feet will take root.

Then
In the terrible mid-day heat
You'll get still
Crayons will appear
And people will show up
To sit
 In the sweet cool shade
Of your shadow
As you color away
In the bright, bright sunlight
Like there's no tomorrow.

15

CLOSURE

Your Story

This book ends with your story. It's the story of your own Heart Awakening. It exists within the larger context that we are all waking up with you. Everything you need to continue Heart Awakening is included within your story. As you probably already know, your story ends happily. Fortunately, and ultimately, there is no other kind of ending.

Congratulations in advance!

Circle Wisdom

In the larger reality, "heart circles" exist wherever there are two or more people opening their hearts to each other in kindness. These circles are as old as our species and they will continue throughout time. We evolve around and towards the opening of the heart. It is why we are here. It is the common human task that unites us.

Heart Circle is designed to make conscious and intentional what already happens when we are led by the longing to awaken with one another. It's a social tool created to support us in becoming more aware of the unlimited possibilities that exist when we come together to cooperate and co-create.

Much of the insanity we are seeing around us today stems from the fact that we are transitioning to a higher-functioning, heart-directed paradigm, while our mass culture is still operating from a fear-based, survival paradigm. As we evolve into something more sensible and sustainable, this transition may come with upheaval, violence, and suffering on its way out. There is no blame here, only rampant disconnection from our collective wisdom.

Dangerous times dramatically reflect back to us the kind of choices we're making daily. Are we frozen in shock or alive in love? Are we in denial, or seeing clearly? Are we living the great *Getaway* or the great *Giveaway*? These times *are* dangerous. There are scary dragons everywhere we look. But dragons give a face to fear, so we can see our fear more clearly.

Moving past fear allows us to be tide pools of peace, serving those caught in tidal waves of change.

Leaving the old paradigm of separation, struggle, and survival and entering into a new paradigm of unity, cooperation, and flow requires two things: *ways of being* that allow us to awaken our hearts, and *strong social groups* that support us in awakening. Heart Circle is one way to work with both of these simultaneously.

Everything I've written in this book leads to one closing question: Do you want to start your own Heart Circle? If you do, I hope this book will serve you!

Whether we have met or not, I'm grateful for the privilege of being in this intimate exploration of possibility with you. I hope the conversation between us continues over time and beyond time, through our common intention to gather together in ever greater awareness and love.

Thank you!

I am complete.

Tej Steiner

DEDICATION

Thanks to all of you with whom I've sat in circle over these past several decades. May this book in some way reflect back to you the positive effect you have had on me and the development of Heart Circle, be it great or small.

I also want to thank you, Mary Londos and Heather Williams. You understood that this book could only come through my willingness to stay open to what the long process of writing it had to teach me. Thank you for your encouragement to keep going and to go deeper, for your many, many hours of discussion and holding space, and most of all, for your feminine wisdom and love which wove themselves deeply into these pages.

And finally, thanks to those of you who have just read this book now or who will do so in the future. I am grateful for your willingness to explore this new transformational circle paradigm with me.

May our hearts continue to open together as we respond to these times with clarity, presence, integrity, love and courage.

TEJ STEINER is a pioneer in using the ancient wisdom circle for personal and social transformational support. A circle facilitator for forty years, he is the founder of Men in Circle and In My Village. He's also the creator of Heart Circle—a process currently used by awakening people around the world. He lives in Ashland, Oregon.

• • •

HEART CIRCLE SUPPORT

For information on Heart Circle workshops or for sponsoring Heart Circle sessions within your family, community or organization, please contact us at connect@heartcircle.com or go to www.heartcircle.com.

Made in the USA
Lexington, KY
15 July 2017